Independent TOEFL Essay Strategies

With Exercises and 90 Essays Scored by an ETS Reader

Roberta G. Steinberg

TABLE OF CONTENTS

Description of Writing Tasks	1
Essay Topics	2
Essay Rating/Writing Scoring Guide	3
Preparation for Writing the Independent Essay	5
A. The Structure and Writing of the Independent Essay	5
I. What an Essay Looks Like/Its Format	5
II. Brainstorming	6
• Brainstorming Strategies	6
• Brainstorming Exercise	7
III. Introduction/Thesis Statement	9
• Introductory Paragraph Strategies	9
• Thesis Statements	9
• Thesis Statement Strategies	9
• Thesis Statement Exercise	10
• Introductory Exercise	10
• Introduction and Thesis Statement Exercise	11
IV. Choosing One Side or Combining Agree/Disagree	12
• Combining and Agree/Disagree Strategies	13
• Combining Agree/Disagree Exercise	13
V. Topic Sentences/Supporting Idea/Transitions	15
• Topic Sentences	15
• Topic Sentences Strategies	16
• Supporting Ideas	16
• Supporting Ideas Strategies	16
• Topic Sentences/Supporting Ideas Exercises	16
• Transitions	19
• Punctuation Rules For Transitions	22
• Transition Strategy	22
• Transition Exercises	23

VI. Conclusions	25
• Conclusion Strategies	25
• Conclusion Exercise	25
VII. Sentence Variety	26
• Sentence Variety Strategies	27
• Sentence Variety Exercise	27
VIII. Including a Title	28
• Title Exercises	29
IX. Editing	31
Preparing for the Essay Strategies	**31**
B. Specific Areas for Grammar Review and Editing	**32**
1. Fragments and Run-on Sentences	32
• Fragment and Run-on Sentences Exercises	33
2. Parallelism	35
• Word Forms/Word Endings	38
• Word Form Exercise	41
• Word Order in Sentences	42
• Parallelism Exercises	42
3. Punctuation	46
• Punctuation Exercise	48
C. Student Essays	**49**
Exercises Answer Key	**129**
Student Essay Scores and Explanations	**137**

This textbook is dedicated to my TOEFL takers from around the world, my husband Avishai Shafrir, and my children, Doree and Michael Shafrir and Karen Vladeck, whose support of my international students over the years has been greatly appreciated.

Robby Steinberg, Boston, Massachusetts, USA

Feel free to email me your comments and questions: rgsteinberg@mountida.edu

Description of Writing Tasks

In the Writing Section you will write type **two essays** on a computer. The first essay is called the *Independent Task*. You will have thirty minutes to prepare, write, and revise a minimum of 300 words on an essay topic from personal experience, not from given material (a reading passage and lecture). The second essay is called the *Integrated Task*. You will first read a 250-300 word passage in 3 minutes and then hear approximately a 2-minute, 230-300 word lecture on the same topic. The information is related, but it does not repeat. You will take notes on the information in each part, and then you will have 20 minutes to prepare, write, and revise a 150-225 word response about how the information is related. In contrast to the *Independent Task*, the *Integrated Task* does NOT ask for your opinion. **This text prepares you to write the Independent Task successfully.**

The essay topic will be given to you. You will have 30 minutes to write on that topic, and that topic only. If you write on any other topic, you will receive a score of "0." The essay topic will appear on the computer screen and will look like this one:

The directions, with a sample topic, are as follows:

Read the topic below and then make any notes that will help you plan your response. Begin typing your response in the box at the bottom of the screen, or write your answer on the answer sheet provided to you.

> *Some people believe that university students should be required to attend classes. Others believe that going to classes should be optional for students. Which point of view do you agree with? Use specific reasons and details to explain your answer.*

At the end of 30 minutes, the computer will automatically end the session.

REMEMBER: You MUST plan, write, and edit in 30 minutes.

I. Essay Topics

ETS publishes a list of writing topics, one of which will probably appear on the actual test (see current TOEFL Bulletin). ETS may add or delete to this list at any time. The most recent bulletin includes 4 different types of essays, which are explained below.

1. Compare/contrast; Agree/disagree (89 such topics listed in Bulletin, or 67% of all questions)
In this kind of essay, you will be asked to compare how two thoughts, ideas, or proposals are similar or how they are different. You can do either or both. You will need to choose which idea you agree with or which one you think is better. In the response to the following question, you could talk about someone you know whose pet has brought them much happiness. Or you could discuss the fact that although people may treat their pets in a ridiculous manner, spending much money on dog clothes and expensive toys, sometimes people have a better life because of a pet.
EXAMPLE: *Many people have a close relationship with their pets. These people treat their birds, cats, or other animals as members of their family. In your opinion, are such relationships good? Why or why not? Use specific reasons and examples to support your answer.*

2. Describe something (21 topics, or 16% of all questions)
In this type of essay, you are asked to describe something. Although the question does not ask you to compare anything, sometimes a comparison helps to make your point.
In response to the following question, you could discuss one country's films and what you learned about the country from them. Or you could contrast how another country's films were so different from your country's films because that other country is so different from your own.
EXAMPLE: *Films can tell us a lot about the country in which they were made. What have you learned about a country from watching its movies? Use specific examples and details to support your answer.*

3. Choose among several choices (20 topics, or 15% of all questions)
In this kind of essay, you will have several different ideas to consider. You will need to choose which one you think is best/most important. You can choose one feature and write your essay on only that (such as location is the most important feature), or you can discuss several different choices before picking the most important one.
EXAMPLE: *When choosing a place to live, what do you consider most important: location, size, style, number of rooms, types of rooms, or other features. Use reasons and specific examples to support your answer.*

4. Make one change to something (3 topics, or fewer than 1% of all questions)
In this type of essay, you will need to analyze the changes you would make to something such as a town, school, or organization. This question is asking you to spend the essay talking about only one choice.
EXAMPLE: *If you could change one thing about your hometown, what would you change? Use reasons and specific examples to support your answer.*

II. Essay Rating

The essay you compose in the Writing section will be scored by two readers using the Writing Score Guide explained below. Neither reader will know the rating assigned by the other. Your essay will receive the average of the two ratings unless there is a discrepancy of more than one point; in that case, a third reader will independently rate your essay. Thus, your essay will receive a final rating 5, 4.5, 4, 3.5, 3, 2.5, 2, 1.5, or 1. A score of 0 will be given to papers that are blank, simply copy the topic, are written in a language other than English, consist only of random keystroke characters, or are written on a topic other than the one assigned.

Writing Scoring Guide

5 An essay at this level accomplishes all of the following:

- effectively addresses the topic and task
- is well organized and well developed, using clearly appropriate explanations, examples, and/or details
- displays unity, progression, and cohesion
- displays consistent facility in the use of language, demonstrating syntactic variety, appropriate word choice and idiom usage, though it may have minor lexical or grammatical errors

Although it may seem as though only a native speaker can write a 5 essay, a 5 essay can have some errors. However, this essay is almost error-free, uses many specific examples, is well-developed in numerous paragraphs, and uses many different English structures. Its length is always close to 300 words.

4 An essay at this level largely accomplishes all of the following:

- addresses the topic and task well, though some points may not be foully elaborated
- is generally well organized and well developed, using appropriate and sufficient explanations, examples, and/or details
- displays unity, progression, and cohesion, though it may be somewhat repetitive, digress, or contain unclear connections
- demonstrates facility in the use of language, uses syntactic variety and a range of vocabulary although it will probably have occasional noticeable errors in structure, word form, or idiomatic language that do not interfere with meaning

This essay is not as developed as a 5, has more errors, but is still a well-written, well-argued piece of writing.

3 An essay at this level is marked by one or more of the following:

- addresses the writing topic using somewhat developed explanations, examples, and/or details
- displays unity, progression, and coherence, although connection of ideas may be occasionally unclear
- may demonstrate inconsistent facility in sentence formation and word choice that may result in lack of clarity and occasionally unclear meaning
- may display accurate but limited range of syntactic structures and vocabulary

An essay 3 writer may one day write a 4 or 5 essay, but for the moment, this writer is strikingly less sophisticated than those who can write a 4 or a 5. There are many areas of weakness: underdeveloped paragraphs or arguments, phrase or word choices that confuse the reader, and numerous grammatical errors.

2 An essay at this level may reveal one or more of the following weaknesses:

- limited development in response to the topic and task
- inadequate organization or connection of ideas
- inappropriate or insufficient examples, explanations, or details to support or illustrate generalizations in response to the task
- a noticeably inappropriate choice of words or word forms
- an accumulation of errors in sentence structure and/or usage

A 2 essay is usually very short. Although it may sometimes have a bright spot (a good argument or some good vocabulary, etc.), overall, it's dramatically less coherent and filled with many more errors than a 3 essay.

1 An essay at this level is seriously flawed by one or more or the following weaknesses:

- serious disorganization or underdevelopment
- little or no detail, or irrelevant specifics, or questionable responsiveness to the task
- serious and frequent errors in sentence structure and usage

Sometimes differentiating between a 1 and a 2 essay is difficult. The 1 essay is generally shorter and much more incomprehensible than a 2.

0 An essay will be rated 0 if it

- contains no response
- merely copies the topic
- is off-topic, is written in a foreign language, or consists only of keystroke characters, or is blank

This score is self-explanatory

III. Preparation for Writing the Independent Essay

This section is divided into three parts: **A: The Structure and Writing of the Independent Essay; B: Specific Areas for Grammar Review and Editing; C: Sample Student Essays** (that have been scored by official readers)

A. The Structure and Writing of the Independent Essay

I.   What an Essay Looks Like/ Its Format
II. Brainstorming (Identifying Main Ideas)
III. Introductions/Thesis Statements
IV. Choosing One Side or Combining Agree/Disagree
V.   Topic Sentences/Supporting Ideas/Transitions
VI. Conclusions
VII. Sentence Variety
VIII. Including a Title
IX. Editing
X.   Suggestions for Preparing for the Essay/Timing

I. What an Independent Essay Looks Like

The **format** of an essay is how looks on a computer screen. It is important to use the correct format.

Vocabulary: Indentations, Paragraphs, Title

INDENTATIONS

All paragraphs must be indented, that means you must leave an inch space on the left-hand side of the margin. When using a regular computer, you can press "Tab" and the computer automatically indents, or goes in, five spaces. When you use the computer for the exam, however, you will have to hit the space bar five times because the tab key does not work in this program. Another suggestion is to leave two lines between paragraphs and don't indent.

PARAGRAPHS

A **paragraph** is a group of sentences that are about one topic. They are connected to the **topic sentence** (see Part V). There should be no unrelated sentences, examples, or ideas in each paragraph. The last sentence of a paragraph should bring it to a logical end. As a general rule, a paragraph should be at least 4 sentences. If your paragraphs are too long (more than 10 sentences), the reader can lose interest.

A standard essay should have at least four paragraphs: one, the introduction and thesis statement; two, the first main point and examples; three, the next major point and its arguments; and four, a conclusion.

Sometimes the essay can have five paragraphs if you have another major point with its supporting specifics. But in 30 minutes you probably won't have enough time to write five developed paragraphs. If you do NOT divide your essay into paragraphs, even if you include all of the points listed above, you will be penalized in the grading of your essay because it does not look like a typical American essay.

II.   Brainstorming

The word comes from "brain" and "storm." As you can guess, the meaning of this word is to generate suddenly many ideas (like an unexpected storm). In order to come up with some ideas quickly before you begin writing, you will need to get good at brainstorming. **TIME: Plan to spend 2-4 minutes brainstorming BEFORE you begin to write.** You will be given scrap paper to use.

BRAINSTORMING STRATEGIES
- **Once you see your question, plan to brainstorm for 2-4 minutes before you write your essay.**
- **Some students close their eyes while thinking of specific points.**
- **Others immediately write down words that come into their minds.**
- **DO NOT write down entire sentences; this time should be used only for MAIN IDEAS.**
- **The purpose of this time is to come up with enough specific points and examples that will prove what your essay is arguing (your thesis statement).**
- **Without supporting details, you cannot prove your thesis statement.**
- **Never begin to write without thinking and writing down key ideas first.**

For example, suppose the question is

Some high schools require all students to wear school uniforms. Other high schools permit students to decide what to wear to school. Which of these two school policies do you think is better? Use specific reasons and example to support your opinion.

Maybe you don't have an opinion about whether or not to require school uniforms when you read this question. So, while brainstorming make two columns and start to think:

FOR	AGAINST
• Cheap-don't need many outfits	• Look like everyone else
• Quicker in AM	• Can't show originality
• No competition	
• Promotes equality	

If you have trouble thinking of reasons not to have uniforms, your thesis statement and essay will be something about how it's better to wear uniforms. You may decide to argue only for wearing uniforms, or you may decide to combine both sides (a more sophisticated essay). Combining opposing ideas will be discussed later. At least now you know what your main points are, and you can begin to think about the examples and stories that will support your points. The key is to decide QUICKLY what side you're taking (even if it's not something you really believe), so that you can begin finding examples and start to write.

BRAINSTORMING EXERCISE

For each question, spend 3-4 minutes coming up with main points.

1. *Some people prefer to spend most of their time alone. Others like to be with friends most of the time. Do you prefer to spend your time alone or with friends? Give reasons to support your answer.*

(You can either **PICK ONE** and see how many points you can find, or you can **LOOK AT BOTH CHOICES** and then see which list is longer.)

ALONE	WITH FRIENDS
1.	1.
2.	2.
3.	3.

2. *A gift (such as a soccer ball, a camera, or an animal) can contribute to a child's development. What gift would you give to help a child develop? Why? Use reasons and specific details to support your choice.*

(This question is asking you to pick only **one**, so quickly choose **one of the choices** and find reasons why that **one** is good.)

SOCCER BALL	CAMERA	ANIMAL
1.	1.	1.
2.	2.	2.
3.	3.	3.

3. *Imagine that you have received some land to use as you wish. How would you use this land? Use specific details to explain your answer.*

(There is no choice in this question, so once you decide what you want to do with the land, write down some benefits for this choice.)

Land Use: _____
Why it's a good choice:
1.

2.

3.

4. **People behave differently when they wear different clothes. Do you agree that different clothes influence the way people behave? Use specific example to support your answer.**

(If you said people don't behave differently, you'd have no essay. List different situations that people act differently in, depending on what they're wearing. Find at least two different situations in which people act differently, and then find specific examples.)

SITUATION 1:_____   SITUATION 2:_____
1.   1.

2.   2.

5. *The 21st century is in its second decade. What changes do you think this new century will bring? Use examples and details in your answer.*

CHANGES
1.

2.

3.

(To make your point, think of specific examples **BEFORE** you starts to write. It's always **BEST** to use **specific examples** whenever you can.)

III. **Introductions/Thesis Statements**

The **introduction** is probably the most important part of the essay. Readers need to decide very quickly what score to give the essay, so they are greatly influenced by what they read first. As you are writing the **introduction**, DO NOT rewrite any part of the question. If you do so, the reader judges that you are a beginning writer and cannot write your own ideas.

INTRODUCTORY PARAGRAPH STRATEGIES
- Make sure it's a paragraph and not just one sentence.
- Give a general introduction-not specifics- to points you will bring up later.
- Think about **sentence variety**, for the introduction is the place to impress the reader. For example, you can ask a question. (see Section VII)
- End the introduction with your **thesis statement**. (see below)

THESIS STATEMENTS: An essay must have a **thesis statement**, the one sentence that tells the reader your point of view. The reader will be convinced that your thesis and essay are good once all of your evidence and specifics are read. As a general rule, put the **thesis statement** last in the opening paragraph. If this paragraph were a play in a theater, the opening sentence se the state, and then in the **thesis statement** we meet the actors.

THESIS STATEMENT STRATEGIES
- A thesis should make the reader want to read the essay.
- A thesis must express an idea with which it is possible to disagree.
- A thesis must express a judgment, an observation, OR a question which the essay will go on to prove.

Here is a question:
> *Some people think they can learn better by themselves than with a teacher. Others think that is it always better to have a teacher. Which do you prefer? Use specific reasons to develop your essay.*

When writing a comparison/contrast essay, try to avoid a thesis statement such as *"There are many advantages to learning by oneself."* because it restates "learn" and "by themselves/oneself" which are in the question and it uses "advantages." Many students write "There are many advantages" or "There are many disadvantages." Readers get tired of reading the same phrases again and again.
- One suggestion is to use the comparative form of the adjective:

Learning by oneself is more beneficial (or productive, satisfying), than learning with a teacher.

Or, depending on the point, you may also use an adverb as a comparison:

Learning by oneself regularly rather than with a teacher eliminates the need to go to school.
- When you are combining opposing points you can use "although":

Although it may seem that learning by oneself is better than with a teacher, it may not always be true.

THESIS STATEMENT EXERCISE

Try to write thesis statements for these questions using comparatives.

1. *Do you agree or disagree with the following statement? Playing a game is fun only when you win.*

2. *Would you prefer to live in a traditional house or in a modern apartment building?*

3. *Do you agree with the following statement? A zoo has no useful purpose.*

4. *Do you agree or disagree with the following statement? All students should be required to study art and music in high school.*

5. *People listen to music for different reasons and at different times. Why is music important to many people?*

6. *People recognize a difference between children and adults. What events (experiences or ceremonies) make a person an adult? Use specific reasons and examples to explain your answer.*

7. *Imagine that you have received some land to use as you wish. How would you use this land? Use specific details to explain your answer.*

INTRODUCTION EXERCISE

Look at this question:

> ***Do you agree or disagree with the following statement? Playing games teaches us about life. Use specific reasons and examples to support your answer.***

What are some of the problems with the following introductions?

1. I agree with the statement that playing games teaches us about life. My essay will explain why I agree.

2. I have always played lots of games, both in school and with my friends. I agree that playing games teaches us about life because it teaches us cooperation, teamwork, and problem-solving skills.

3. When I was in high school I played soccer every day. I had to learn how to get along with my teammates and balance my homework with practice. I couldn't go to parties on the weekends, couldn't smoke, and had to watch my diet.

4. What makes this introduction different?

   There are many kinds of games. For some people, participating in athletic games is a major part of their lives whereas other people spend hours every day playing video games or board games. Others like doing word games such as crossword puzzles. Playing games can take up a lot of time, but can playing games teach us something? Playing soccer has taught me life lessons that I would not have learned otherwise.

INTRODUCTION AND THESIS STATEMENT EXERCISE

Look at these questions and write introductions and thesis statements for them.

1. Some people say that advertising encourages us to buy things we really do not need. Others say that advertisements tell us about new products that may improve our lives. Which viewpoint do you agree with? Use specific reasons and examples to support your answer.

2. What is the most important animal in your country? Why is this animal important? Use reasons and specific details to explain your answer.

3. Choose a building that has special meaning for you. Explain why this building is important to you. Support your explanation with specific details.

IV.   Choosing One Side or Combining Agree/Disagree

Since 67 percent of all questions ask you to agree or disagree with a statement, you should spend time thinking about how you want to write about this kind of essay. Many argue that it's easier to pick one side in a prompt and write the essay only arguing for that point. For example, look at this question.

> *Some people believe that students should be given one long vacation each year. Others believe that students should have several short vacations throughout the year. Which viewpoint do you agree with? Use specific reasons and examples to support your choice.*

It may seem that you need only decide whether you prefer one long or several short vacations. You certainly could write a well-argued essay for one choice. But carefully consider looking at both sides. Because there isn't a right/wrong answer, often a more sophisticated essay is able to include a discussion of **BOTH** options and explain why the decision isn't simply one or the other. There may be times when you would want several short vacations and another time you would like one long one. If you decide to choose only one side, the reader may be left feeling you haven't carefully thought about the question.

Your thesis statement could look something like this:
Although I appreciate the sense of relaxation a long vacation can give me, several short vacations are very much needed during a stressful academic year.

One paragraph would discuss how great it is to have a long vacation, using a specific long vacation that you took and how great it made you feel. The next paragraph would talk about the benefits of several short vacations during the year, again using some personal stories that demonstrate the value of this type of vacationing.

Here's another question, which asks you compare and contrast two different ideas. It may seem that you are being asked to choose only one idea. But by incorporating both sides into an argument, you are creating a more advanced essay.

> *It has been said, "Not everything that is learned is contained in books." Compare and contrast knowledge from experience with knowledge gained from books. In your opinion, which source is more important?*

First brainstorm both sides:

From experience
- What friends/family have been through
- Learning on my own (riding a bike)

From books
- Technical info couldn't get elsewhere
- "How to books" info from experts

Since there are arguments for both sources, the thesis statement could be something like this

I have learned many things from books; however, sometimes what I have learned from my own experiences has been just as important.

One paragraph would be about all the technical things you learned from books: how to install computer programs, how to prepare for the TOEFL, how to make lasagna. The next paragraph would detail what you learned from your own and others' experiences: how to ride a bike, how to hold a baby, how to do some task at a job. The conclusion would incorporate both ideas: a recipe you found of how to make lasagna but only through your own experience of cooking it and speaking to others who cook it were you able to perfect it.

COMBINING and AGREE/DISAGREE STRATEGIES
- **Brainstorm each prompt, making sure you have points for both sides.**
- **Make sure your thesis statement includes a transition that shows contrast.**
- **Your thesis statement can clearly state that you agree with a combination of both sides or under certain circumstances you agree with each side.**
- **Then one paragraph will look at one side; the next will look at the other.**
- **Or, you may use both paragraphs to combine the ideas (a little bit harder to do).**
- **Make sure the conclusion restates why and in what circumstances you agree with both sides.**

COMBINING AGREE/DISAGREE EXERCISE

Look at these prompts. Brainstorm for a few minutes then write a thesis statement that includes both sides, using a transition that shows contrast.

1. *Some people prefer to spend time with one or two close friends. Others choose to spend time with a large number of friends. Compare the advantages of each choice. Which of these two ways of spending time do you prefer? Give reasons to support your answer.*

One or two friends	**A large number of friends**
1.	1.
2.	2.
3.	3.

Thesis statement: _____

_____.

2. *Some people believe that a college or university education should be available to all students. Others believe that higher education should be available only to good students. Discuss these views. Which view do you agree with? Explain why.*

All students	**Good Students only**
1.	1.
2.	2.
3.	3.

Thesis statement: _____

_____.

3. *Some people prefer to spend their free time outdoors. Other people prefer to spend their leisure time indoors. Would you prefer to be outside or would you prefer to be inside for your leisure activities? Use specific reasons and example to support your choice.*

Outdoors	**Indoors**
1.	1.
2.	2.
3.	3.

Thesis statement: _____

_____.

4. *Do you agree or disagree with the following statement? People should sometimes do things that they do not enjoy doing.*

Should do	**Shouldn't do**
1.	1.
2.	2.
3.	3.

Thesis statement: _____

_____.

5.   *Some items (such as clothes or furniture) can be made by hand or by machine. Which do you prefer-items made by hand or items made by machine? Use reasons and specific examples to explain your choice.*

By hand	**By machine**
1.	1.
2.	2.
3.	3.

Thesis statement:_____

_____.

V.   Topic Sentences/Supporting Idea/Transitions

Topic Sentences

The topic sentence directs the reader by telling what the paragraph is trying to argue/prove. Each of the two paragraphs in the body of your essay should have a topic sentence. Although a topic sentence can come anywhere in the paragraph, it often is the first sentence in the paragraph because it makes it clear to the reader what will follow. In addition, the writer can keep looking back to make sure that all the sentences in that paragraph are related to that sentence.

For example, if your paragraph were discussing salaries of athletes and movie stars, a topic sentence could be *Many athletes and entertainers make more than doctors, lawyers, and even presidents.* You could then go on to contrast some specific people, their salaries, and their responsibilities.

Or if your paragraph is describing the benefits of wearing a uniform a topic sentence could be *Wearing a uniform made my life in high school easy.* You would then discuss the specific ways it helped you.

Or if you were discussing the benefits of zoos your topic sentence could be *Many animals would now be extinct if we didn't have zoos.* You would then name several species that are not extinct because zoos have protected them, enabling them to reproduce.

TOPIC SENTENCES STRATEGIES
- It briefly states an idea that is more fully developed in the paragraph with examples and specifics.
- If you put your topic sentence at the beginning, you can quickly look up as you write to remind yourself what you're focus is.
- Checking the topic sentence as you write helps keep you from putting in ideas that are not connected.
- The topic sentence should be the main idea of the paragraph, not the specifics.
- Try not to make it too general, for it needs to state the focus of the paragraph.
- The ideas in the topic sentences come from the thesis statement.

Supporting Ideas
The supporting ideas prove and support what your topic sentence claims. When you brainstorm, you wrote down specific examples or experiences that you can now use.

SUPPORTING IDEAS STRATEGIES
- The supporting ideas often include your own experiences and observations.
- The TOEFL essay assumes you'll be talking about yourself. These personal experiences and stories make your writing richer and can prove your point. Don't worry if these points seem too conversational or personal. It is expected that you will write about yourself.
- Each supporting idea needs several sentences to develop, so the first sentence after the topic sentence can introduce the specific example/story you're about to write.

TOPIC SENTENCE/SUPPORTING IDEAS EXERCISE 1

I. Here's a question we looked at earlier:

Read and think about the following statement. People behave differently when they wear different clothes. Do you agree that different clothes influence the way people behave? Use specific examples to support your answer.

Brainstorming ideas could look like this:

Dressed up
- Act differently
- Feel more grown up
- Doing something special

Wearing a Uniform
- Behave differently
- Commands respect
- Can instill fear

A thesis statement could look like this:
Whenever I'm wearing clothes that I don't usually wear, such as formal clothes or a uniform I behave differently and people act differently to me.

For each pair of sentences, decide which is the better topic sentence and which is the better supporting point.

1. Wearing a uniform makes the wearer feel different.
   When I put on my school uniform, I know I'm going to school.

2. People act differently when they see people wearing uniforms.
   When I see a policeman in uniform, I get scared.

3. Wearing a long dress and high heels makes me feel glamorous.
   Getting dressed up can change how I act and feel.

4. In my country, people get dressed up on special occasions.
   Every birthday party my friends and I celebrate by wearing our best clothes.

5. I didn't think that how I dressed made a difference.
   Our speech teacher made us dress up on speech days.

II. Find two or three points that can support the following topic sentences:

1. Some people think young children should spend most of their time playing.

-
-
-

2. Some people think that children should begin their formal education at a very early age and should spend most of their time on school studies.

-
-
-

III. Which sentence is better as sentence #2 in a paragraph, and which one would be better as sentence #3?

1. A. By studying Farsi, you will be able to learn about an entirely different people and history.
   B. Once you are able to read Farsi poetry, you will understand the Persian people's struggle for independence.

2. A. A movie theater would give people of all ages a place to go for entertainment.
   B. My hometown doesn't have a movie theater.

3. A. Whenever I'm feeling sad, I put on a CD and listen to Chopin.
    B. Music can change my moods.

4. A. A dog can help any child feel better about herself.
    B. My parents got me a dog when I was eleven.

5. A. Some people don't understand how a pet can be like a family member.
    B. Every year we have a party for Moomoo, our pet parrot.

TOPIC SENTENCE/SUPPORTING DETAILS EXERCISE 2

A common problem is using details that don't really support, or logically follow your topic sentences. **In the following exercise, choose and explain which set of details (A) or (B) more logically support the topic sentence.**

1. Topic Sentence: The 21st century will bring many medical changes.

(A) There will be cures for diseases such as AIDS and cancer.
    Doctors will rely more on computers to treat and diagnose patients.
    Better medical care will result in people living longer.

(B) There aren't enough doctors in my country.
    Most people can't afford to buy the pills they need to take.
    The hospitals don't have enough supplies to treat their patients.

2. Topic Sentence: I would buy a business rather than a house.

(A) I would love to live near the ocean.
    Houses aren't as expensive in my country as they are in the U.S.
    Having my own business will take up all my time.

(B) If my business is successful, I would be able to buy a house one day.
    It's not so important to me where I live.
    I've always dreamed of having my own business.

3. Topic Sentence: Once I had to borrow money from a friend in order to pay my rent.

(A) I thought my best friend would lend me the money.
    I knew my friend was worried I wouldn't pay him back.
    I didn't want to lose this friend, so I quickly paid him back.

(B) My rent is due on the first of the month.

I have many friends who have lots of money in the bank.
It's cheaper to live in an apartment than in the dorm.

4. Topic Sentence: Music is important to me because it helps me relax.

(A) I've always loved to sing.
I listen to the radio when I'm studying.
Some of my friends borrow my CDs because I have so many good ones.

(B) After a hard day, I put on the radio and feel better.
When I have a headache, I listen to Bach.
It's hard to explain, but listening to music makes me forget my problems.

Transitions
Transitions are words that join one idea to another idea. We use transitions *within* a paragraph as well as *between* paragraphs. Transitions help the reader follow from one idea to the next. These words are also known as *connectors, markers,* or *signal words.*

I. To Show Addition

A. **Positive**	B. **Negative**	C. **Series**
- and	neither…nor	first (ly)…second(ly)
- as well	nor	next
- also	neither	lastly, finally
- too		
- moreover		
- furthermore		
- in addition		
- what's more		
- similarly		

II. To Show Example
- for example
- such as
- for instance

III. To Show Similarity
- similarly
- likewise
- in the same way
- as….as
- as in, as with, as was etc.

III. To Show Cause or Reason
- because (of)

- due to
- on account of
- thanks to
- since
- for this reason
- as a result
- caused by

IV. To Show Effect or Result
- as a result
- consequently
- thereby
- thus

V. To Show Conclusion/Summary
- therefore
- hence
- in conclusion
- thus
- to sum up
- at last
- finally
- all in all
- as a result
- in summary/to summarize
- in brief
- on the whole
- to conclude

VI. To Show Contrast
- in contrast
- on the contrary
- in fact
- however
- yet
- although/even though
- on the one hand….on the other hand
- nevertheless/nonetheless
- whereas
- unlike
- despite
- in spite of
- even so
- instead

- despite
- but
- rather than
- either…or

VII.   To Show Emphasis
- clearly
- evidently
- obviously
- actually
- in fact
- indeed
- surely
- above all
- certainly
- definitely
- extremely
- absolutely
- positively
- surprisingly
- unquestionably
- without a doubt
- objectively

VIII.   To Show Purpose
- so that
- so as to
- in order to

IX.   To Show Restatement/Repetition
- that is
- in other words
- to put it differently
- to repeat
- namely

X.   To Set Up a Condition
- if
- even if
- whether (or not)
- may/might
- can be

XI. To Show Time Relationships
- immediately
- then
- later
- afterwards
- after
- before
- while
- during
- as soon as
- sometimes
- lastly
- frequently
- when
- once
- often/oftentimes

Punctuation Rules for Transitions:

I. Sentences with coordinating conjunction (*for, and, nor, but or, yet, so*)
You can remember all of these words by taking the first letter of each word and making it into the word "FANBOYS." If you have an independent clause (a subject + verb that can stand alone) that is connected to another independent clause with a FANBOYS, put a (,) before the FANBOYS.

Example: Colleges should give money to students' sports activities, but they should spend the same amount on their libraries.

II. Sentences can begin with TRANSITONAL (or CONJUNCTIVE) ADVERBS (such as *however, therefore, nonetheless, nevertheless, moreover, in fact, hence, consequently, in addition, thus*). If these words connect 2 independent clauses, the punctuation is (;) transitional adverb (,).

Example: I think it's a good idea for students to evaluate teachers; however, I think most students would be afraid to tell what they really think.

III. Adverbial clauses that begin with subordinating conjunctions (if, because, although, time words=when, after, before, etc.) need a comma after the clause. There is no comma if the clause is at the end of the sentence.

Example: If a shopping center is built in my neighborhood, I'd be really happy.
I'd be really happy if a shopping center is built in my neighborhood.

TRANSITION STRATEGY
- **Try to introduce new paragraphs and especially the conclusion with a transition.**

TRANSITION EXERCISES

I. Finish these sentences.

1. Some people prefer to spend most of their time alone; however,

   _____.

2. A zoo has no useful purpose. In other words,

   _____.

3. Playing games encourages cooperation, teamwork, and problem-solving skills; therefore,_____.

4. Students should evaluate their teachers so that_____.

5. Building a shopping center in my neighborhood would cause many problems. For example,_____

6. I learn better with a teacher due to

   _____.

7. Advertising encourages us to buy things we really do not need; furthermore,,

   _____.

8. The most important class I ever took was my ESL class; consequently,

   _____.

9. I would prefer to live in a modern apartment building. Similarly,

   _____.

10. All students should be required to study art and music in high school. Indeed,

    _____.

II. Choose the correct transition for each sentence.

1. _____ my high school teacher, I applied to study in the United States.
   a. namely   b. as well   c. thanks to   d. all in all

2. Some athletes make millions of dollars every year for playing games a few hours a week. _____, some doctors who trained for years and years make much less.
   a. In contrast   b. Despite   c. Likewise   d. Even so

3. The most important animal in my country is the camel _____ it can carry loads for many miles without much water.
   a. because   b. because of   c. thus   d. that is

4. First, the kitchen is where I eat. _____, the kitchen is where I do my homework.
   a. Obviously   b. Second   c. In the same way   d. Finally

5. I began studying English as a very young child. _____, it has been easy for me to become fluent.
   a. As a result   b. On the contrary   c. Even so   d. Next

III. Combine the following sentences into ONE sentence using one of the transitions below. Some words can work in more than one sentence.

   moreover   hence   and   although   whereas

1. My favorite class I ever took was my writing class last semester. I had to get up at 6:30 in the morning to get to it on time.

   _____

2. My writing class always gave homework. My reading class never gave homework.

   _____

3. I had to take three buses. I had to walk half a mile to campus.

   _____

4. The writing teacher helped me more than any other teacher I've ever had. I signed up to take another class with her next semester.

   _____

5. I really loved writing essays. I'm thinking about becoming an English major.

   _____

VI. Conclusions

The conclusion is the fourth and final paragraph to your essay. It gives an ending to your essay, so the reader knows you are done. Your conclusion should include a rewording of your thesis statement, so the reader will know that you have proved your argument.

Many people say the closing paragraph of an essay is just as important as the opening one. But the TOEFL is somewhat different. By the time the reader has gotten to your conclusion, he or she has probably decided on what score to give. In general, the conclusion is extremely important because it's the last picture the reader has. On the TOEFL, concentrate more on the introduction. That does not mean that you can omit a conclusion, but spend more time thinking about what you're going to write in the introduction and how you're going to write it.

CONCLUSION STRATEGIES
- **Briefly summarize the main points.**
- **Make sure you restate your thesis statement in light of your arguments. But don't just copy your thesis statement; paraphrase it.**
- **Make it a full paragraph. Give yourself five minutes to make sure you don't run out of time before writing the conclusion.**
- **End with a sentence that readers will remember.**

CONCLUSION EXERCISE

Rewrite these thesis statements trying to use different words.
Example:
Thesis statement: Although it may seem that many people listen to and care about the opinions of famous people such as rock stars, actors, and athletes, what these people have to say is usually not very important.
Rewrite: Nowadays, we hear on television, read in the paper, and see on the Internet what famous singers, movie stars, or athletes think about important issues. I suggest that we listen to and care about what more experienced, learned people have to say.

1. Depending on my mood, I sometimes find reading fiction to be more enjoyable than watching movies.

---

1. When choosing a place to live, I consider the number of rooms to be most important factor.

---

2. Although there are many countries I would like to visit, I would visit Australia if I had the opportunity.

---

3. Some people are satisfied with what they have; however, others always want something more or something different.

4. I've probably seen a million advertisements in my lifetime, but the one that I believe is most effective is the Sony Walkman ad that uses a famous Japanese monkey.

5. If I could change one thing about the school I attended, it would be the dress code.

6. I know that in the United States some high schools allow students to study what they want, but I think that students shouldn't make those decisions.

7. Due to my family's sense of humor, we have all survived some very difficult situations.

9. Whenever I move to a new country, I follow the advice "When in Rome, do as the Romans."

10. What keeps old people young is what they can learn from young people.

VII. Sentence Variety

Using a variety of sentence structures will make your writing more advanced and enjoyable to read. You may be writing sentences that are grammatically correct but boring. As you look over your essays, do all your sentences begin with a SUBJECT + VERB? Do you often connect clauses within your sentence only with AND? As you concentrate on improving your writing, try to change the word order of your sentences.

For example, look at these two simples sentences (SUBJECT + VERB).

I cooked every night at home. I hoped to become a great chef.

You could instead combine them with a *gerund phrase*.
***By* cooking *every night at home*,** I hoped to become a great chef.

Or you could use a *participial phrase*.

Cooking every night, I hoped to become a great chef.

Or you could use an *infinitive phrase*.
My only hope of becoming a great chef was *to cook every night*.

Or you could begin with a *prepositional phrase*.
With nightly home cooked meals, I hoped to become a great chef.

Or you could use an *appositive phrase*.
There was only one way to become a great chef: *nightly home cooked meals*.

Or you could use connectors
Compound sentence: I cooked every night at home, *for I hoped to become a great chef*.
Complex sentence: I cooked every night at home *because I hoped to become a great chef*.

SENTENCE VARIETY STRATEGIES
- **Use an occasional question.**
- **Make sure you're not beginning all sentences with (I + a verb).**
- **Don't write all simple sentences. Look at your writing to see where you could connect two simple sentences into one compound or complex sentence. (This suggestion does NOT mean that your sentences should necessarily be long!)**
- **Use the above-mentioned phrase variations.**

SENTENCE VARIETY EXERCISE

Rewrite and combine these sentences to make them more interesting. Feel free to add words and related ideas.

1. I wore a uniform every day. I hated it.

   _____

2. I've lived in five countries. I tried to dress and act like the native people.

   _____

3. I've learned many things on my own. I learned how to ride a bicycle by riding one, not by reading about it.

   _____

4. In my country, university students don't have to go to class. Teachers don't care whether or not students come.

   _____

5. I played soccer in high school. My team never won one game.

   _____

6. I have many friends and go out with them on the weekend. I like to be alone during the week.

7. I grew up in a modern twenty-two-story apartment building. I want to live in a traditional house.

8. I would visit Australia. I could never afford to go there.

9. Some people listen to music when they are sad. Some people listen to music when they are in a good mood.

10. I live in a very boring small town. I wish we had a movie theater in town.

VIII. Including a Title

You may choose to give your essay a **title**. Writers often choose the title once the essay is finished. An interesting title makes your essay special and makes the reader want to read it. Don't just say *Uniforms* but something such as *Another Day, Another Blue Jumper*. Instead of *Soccer*, try something like *Soccer: Not Just a Game*. Instead of *Films in the U.S.*, try using a question such as *Is America Really Like Its Movies?*

Punctuation Rules for Titles:
- Do not use quotation marks.
- Always capitalize the first word.
- Do not capitalize articles (*a, an, the*), coordinating conjunctions (*for, and, nor, but, or, yet, so*) or prepositions (*in, on, at*, etc.) UNLESS these words are the first word in the title.
- Capitalize all major words such as nouns, pronouns, verbs, adjectives, and adverbs.
- It's OK to ask a question, followed by a question mark.

You do not have to include a title, but if you decide to use one, do not simply repeat the question.
For example, if your question is

Some people prefer to eat at food stands or restaurants. Other people prefer to prepare and eat food at home. Which do you prefer? Use specific reasons and examples to support your answer.

A bad choice of a title would be "Eating at Restaurants." It only restates part of the prompt.

A title should create some interest in the essay. Better choices would be
- Let's Eat Out
- Nothing Beats Home Cooking
- Pizza Again?
- What's for Supper?

All of these choices make the reader want to read the essay.

TITLE EXERCISES

I.   From the following prompts choose the better title and be able to explain why.

1.   Schools should ask students to evaluate their teachers. Do you agree or disagree? Use specific reasons and example to support your answer.

Which title do you prefer and why?
a.   Should students evaluate teachers?
b.   Fear of Teacher Retaliation

2.   Do you agree or disagree with the following statement? A person's childhood (the time from birth to 12 years of age) are the most important years of a person's life. Use specific reasons and details to support your choice.

Which title do you prefer and why?
a.   My Life Began at Thirteen
b.   The Most Important Years

3.   Think of the most important class you have ever taken. Why did you enjoy this class so much? Use specific reason and details to explain your answer.

Which title do you prefer and why?
a.   The Most Important Class
b.   Why I Was Never Absent

4.   You want to persuade someone to study your native language. What reasons would you give? Support your answer with specific details.

Which title do you prefer and why?
a.   A Whole New World
b.   You Should Study Farsi

5.   Many people have a close relationship with their pets. These people treat birds, cats, or other animals as members of their families. In your opinion, are such relationships good? Why or why not? Use specific reasons and examples to support your opinion.

Which title do you prefer and why?
a. My Dog Moomoo
b. You're Invited to Moomoo's Birthday Party

II. **Without first writing an essay, try and create an interesting title that connects to an essay you would write. Be able to explain what makes your title interesting.**

1. *Do you agree or disagree with the following statement? Universities should give the same amount of money to their students' sports activities as they give to the university libraries.*

2. *It has recently been announced that a shopping center may be built in your neighborhood. Do you support or oppose this plan? Why? Use specific reasons and details to support your answer.*

3. *What do you consider to be the most important room in a house? Why is this room more important to you than any other room? Use specific reasons and examples to support you opinion.*

4. *In general, people are living longer now. How will this change affect society? Use specific details and example to develop your essay.*

5. *If you were asked to send one thing representing your country to an international exhibition, what would you choose? Why? Use specific reasons and details to explain your choice.*

6. *Do you agree or disagree with the following statement? A person's childhood (the time from birth to 12 years of age) is the most important time of a person's life. Use specific reasons and details to support your choice.*

7. *Think of the most important class you have ever taken. Why did you enjoy this class so much? Use specific reasons and details to explain your answer.*

8. *You want to persuade someone to study your native language. What reasons would you give? Support your answer with specific details.*

9. Many people have a close relationship with their pets. These people treat birds, cats, or other animals as members of their families. In your opinion, are such relationships good? Why or why not? Use specific reasons and examples to support your opinion.

IX. Editing

As a suggestion, try to leave five minutes at the end of the essay, so you can look it over. At this time, add a title, or quickly notice if you've used one word several times in a paragraph (such as "*interesting*" or "*therefore*") and then change these words. But don't start rewriting the essay or try to add entirely new sentences. If you have only five minutes left and you haven't written a conclusion, it's more important to write one than to reread your essay.

PREPARING FOR THE ESSAY STRATEGIES
- **Get a copy of the TOEFL bulletin and turn to the writing prompts. Set aside a half hour each day for at least a month and write in response to a different prompt each day.**
- **After a short time, you should notice that you're able to write more in 30 minutes than you initially could.**
- **Remember to brainstorm specific points/examples BEFORE you start writing.**
- **Never start typing the essay with the idea of "copying it over."**
- **Have a native English speaker read some of your essays and talk about them with you.**

B. Specific Areas for Grammar Review and Editing

1. FRAGMENTS AND RUN-ON SENTENCES

In writing, two common mistakes are fragments and run-on sentences.

A fragment is an incomplete sentence that does not express a complete thought. It may be missing a subject, a verb, or part of it. It can also be a dependent clause that needs an independent clause.

Example: Because I came to America.
This dependent clause is NOT a sentence because it needs an independent clause to complete its meaning.
Because I came to America, I met many Americans.

Example: More students going to school.
This sentence should read *More students are going to school.*

Example: So for me is very easy to understand Argentinean people.
This sentence should read *So for me it is very easy to understand Argentinean people.*

A run-on error is two or more sentence joins without a word to connect them or comma to connect them. If you put a comma between them, it is still incorrect. This error is called a comma splice.
Example: Sometimes I like to be with one or two friends sometimes I like to be with a large group of friends.

There are 5 ways to correct this run-on.

1.   Make 2 sentences.
Although your sentences will be grammatically correct, this way is not the best. It creates 2 choppy simple sentences instead of one complex one.
Sometimes I like to be with one or two friends. Sometimes I like to be with a large group of friends.

2.   Use a coordinating conjunction (for, and, nor, but, or, yet, so).
Sometimes I like to be with one or two friends, but sometimes I like to be with a large group of friends.

3.   Use a semicolon (;).
You can use a semicolon between 2 closely-related sentences. Be careful not to overuse this punctuation.
Sometimes I like to be with one or two friends; sometimes I like to be with a large group of friends.

4.   Use a transitional adverb (however, therefore, consequently etc).

Be careful of the punctuation. Subject + Verb **; transitional adverb,** subject + verb.
Sometimes I like to be with one or two friends; however; sometimes I like to be with a large group of friends.

5.   Make one a dependent clause.
Although sometimes I like to be with one or two friends, sometimes I like to be with a large group of friends.

Exercise 1

Tell if the following are Sentences (S), Fragments (F) or Run-ons (RO). If F or RO, correct them.

_____ 1. For example, if you're going to buy a watch.

_____ 2. Learning English is not easy, it takes up your time and energy.

_____ 3. A good roommate who is quiet.

_____ 4. Getting out of the city for a camping trip.

_____ 5. My problem is the irregular verbs.

_____ 6. I spent three months looking for an apartment I couldn't find anything under $1000. a month.

_____ 7. Twelve required courses in math and statistics.

_____ 8. What is your major?

_____ 9. A two-week vacation is a very short time to experience another country.

_____ 10. She couldn't understand the directions, she asked her friend for help.

Exercise 2

From these student sentences, tell if the following are Sentences (S), Fragments (FR), or Run-ons (RO). If F or RO, correct them.

_____ 1. First who like to spend time with close friends can do many things in a short time.

_____ 2. I think children should be required to help with household tasks as soon as they are able to do so because parents can give their children some knowledge and include them as family members.

_____ 3. Second, when you are with a large number of friends.

_____ 4. Let me give an example, when I was in the first year of university, I used to be always with two of my friends.

_____ 5. Well, those are my basic points of wanting to go there, I hope that now you understand my desire.

_____ 6. I would probably choose Spain I think that this choice may create confusion with the readers, but I will give my reasons.

_____ 7. Regardless of gender, age, religion, and nationality, a teacher's role in learning is enormous because a teacher is a guide who will help open my eyes to some specific field which it totally unknown.

_____ 8. I prefer to have a teacher because if I learn by myself maybe when I learn something it mistake.

_____ 9. Sometimes when I have problems.

_____ 10. Two reasons.

_____ 11. But with the teachers like computers?

_____ 12. When I was a child, I grew up in the countryside, I think it is a nice place for children's education.

_____ 13. When I saw a fire in the kitchen.

_____ 14. Through their personal experiences such as training.

_____ 15. If I don't have experience about it.

_____ 16. After having said the advantages of one of the other choices and having had the personal experience as an example, I prefer to spend time with one or two close friends than with a large number of friends.

_____ 17. No matter what you think.

_____ 18. Even though unrelated to their occupation in the future.

_____ 19. Because I am a person who can feel nature beautifully, who helps other people, and who knows social rules.

_____ 20. However, sometimes I would like just to be with one or two of my friends rather than with a large number of friends.

2. PARALLELISM

In writing, one must construct a sentence making sure its parts are parallel, or the sentence will be off balance. Always try to balance similar structures, especially in lists, series, or around connecting words within your sentences. In addition, look for faulty parallel construction in the structure section. In order to make sure your writing is parallel, make sure you understand the following points:

A. <u>Connect sentence parts with Coordinating Conjunctions</u>
The word "FANBOYS", which stands for

F=for   A=and   N=nor   B=but   O=or   Y=yet   S=so

will help you remember coordinating conjunctions. These words connect words, phrases, or clauses that have the same grammatical construction.

- A good clause or phrase combines the same kinds of words, phrases, or clauses. Combine a noun with a noun, not a noun with an adjective.

WORDS
1. Noun + Noun
<u>Recession</u> or <u>inflation</u> will lead to disaster.

2. Verb + Verb
-The pharmacist <u>weighed</u> and <u>measured</u> the medicine.

3. Adjective + Adjective
-The child was <u>little</u> yet surprisingly <u>strong</u>.

With three or more items in a series, use commas.
The play was funny, enjoyable, and short.

4.   Adverb + Adverb
-He ran **quickly** but **carefully**.

PHRASES   (groups of words that lack either a subject or a verb)
1.   a(n) + adjective + noun
-He is **a serious student** but **a hilarious comic**.

2.   verb + adverb
-Karen **swims quickly** yet **talks slowly**.

3.   prepositional phrase + prepositional phrase
-David eats **in the morning** and **in the afternoon**.

CLAUSES (groups of words that include a subject and a verb)
1.   adjective clause + adjective clause
-Peter is a colleague **who teaches math** and **who conducts the orchestra**.
2.   noun clause + noun clause
-I know **that you are smart** and **that you are nervous**.

- THERE ARE MANY OTHER TYPES OF WORDS, PHRASES, AND CLAUSES THAT YOU CAN USE IN YOUR WRITING. THESE ARE JUST **SOME** EXAMPLES.

B.   Connect similarly constructed sentences with Paired Conjunctions

- Instead of two short sentences, always try to combine sentences. One good way to connect similarly constructed sentences is with paired conjunctions. The pairs are

   1. Both….and (which takes a plural noun)
-**Both Susan and Jenny speak Chinese.**
   2. Not only…but also
-**Karen not only jogs but also lifts weights.**
   3. Either…or
-**Either the idioms or the phrasal verbs are my biggest problem.**
   4. Neither….nor
-**Neither the football players nor the soccer players can take afternoon classes.**

The subjects that come after the but also, or, and nor determine the verb.
-**Either the teacher or the students erase the blackboard every day.** ("Students" is plural, so the verb "erase" agrees.)
-**Either the students or the teacher erases the blackboard every day.** ("The teacher" is singular, so the verb "erase" agrees.)

- When these pairs are used, they must be followed by parallel types of words, phrases, or clauses. Whenever possible, put as much as you can BEFORE the conjunction.

Here are two choppy sentences, parallelly constructed:

>I want to go to Mexico. I want to go to Brazil.

These sentences can be combined into
-I want to go to both Mexico and Brazil.

INCORRECT: I want both to go Mexico and to Brazil.

Here are two more simple sentences:

>I swim in the morning. If not, I swim at night.

These sentences can be combined into
-I swim either in the morning or at night.

INCORRECT: I swim in either the morning or night. (because "night" takes "at" not "in")

Another two sentences which can be easily combined are
>She knew what to say. She knew when to say it.

These sentences can be combined into
-She knew not only what to say but when to say it.

C.   <u>Do not omit necessary words</u>

- Be careful of changing verb tenses within a sentence.
INCORRECT: I always have and always will eat breakfast.
-I have always eaten and will always eat breakfast.

- Be careful of changing articles within a sentence.
INCORRECT: Mark gave me an apple, pear and oranges.
-Mark gave me an apple, a pear, and oranges.

- Be careful of changing prepositions.
INCORRECT: I was interested and surprised by the story.
-I was interested in and surprised by the story.

- As (which always needs a second "as") and Than

When these two connectives introduce comparisons, you must be sure that the things compared are similar.
INCORRECT: The population of Japan is greater than Korea. DON'T compare a population with a country.
-The population of Japan is greater than that of Korea.

INCORRECT: Joanne is as tall if not taller than her sister. (Although you may hear this sentence in conversation, don't forget the second "as".)
-Joanne is as tall as if not taller than her sister.

WORD FORMS/WORD ENDINGS
In order to make sure the parts of your sentence are parallel, you will need to know what part of speech a word is by its ending. By memorizing suffixes (endings to the roots of words), you will be able to know if a word is used incorrectly.

Memorize the following chart and add in your own examples:

NOUNS	**EXAMPLES**	**YOUR EXAMPLES**
• ness	happiness	_____, _____
• (i)ty	community	_____, _____
• th	width	_____, _____
• sion, tion	position	_____, _____
• ism	Buddhism	_____, _____
• ure	architecture	_____, _____

(ure can also indicate a verb)

• ment	repayment	_____, _____

(ment can also indicate a verb)

• ude	gratitude	_____, _____
• ence, ance	independence	_____, _____
• ship	friendship	_____, _____
• ery, ary	cemetery	_____, _____
• hood	neighborhood	_____, _____
• ory	memory	_____, _____
• phy, gy, try	philosophy	_____, _____
• inct	precinct	_____, _____
• ess	address	_____, _____

(ess can also indicate a verb)

PEOPLE NOUNS
- ist, yst   chemist   _____, _____
- er, or   doctor   _____, _____
- ess   hostess   _____, _____
- ian   librarian   _____, _____
- ic   medic   _____, _____

(ic can also indicate adjectives)
- eur   voyeur   _____, _____
- ant, ent   correspondent   _____, _____
- ect, ict   suspect   _____, _____

(ect/ict can also indicate verbs)

VERBS
- ize (yze)   criticize   _____, _____
- ate   refrigerate   _____, _____

(ate can also indicate adjectives)
- ify   identify   _____, _____
- ete   complete   _____, _____
- uish   distinguish   _____, _____
- ish   finish   _____, _____

(ish can also indicate adjectives)
- en   lengthen   _____, _____
- ute   dilute   _____, _____
- ure   endure   _____, _____
- ose   oppose   _____, _____
- ine   determine   _____, _____
- ulge   indulge   _____, _____
- ict   predict   _____, _____
- erse   converse   _____, _____
- end   pretend   _____, _____
- use   enthuse   _____, _____

- erve   deserve   _____, _____
- uce   produce   _____, _____
- ess   address   _____, _____
- uade, ade   persuade   _____, _____
- ote   promote   _____, _____
- ond   respond   _____, _____
- ave   behave   _____, _____
- age   encourage   _____, _____
- ect   reflect   _____, _____
- ame   inflame   _____, _____
- ment   experiment   _____, _____
- oy   destroy   _____, _____

ADJECTIVES
- ly   _____, _____

(usually _ly signifies an adverb, but some nouns + ly= adjectives)
- less   careless   _____, _____
- ful   useful   _____, _____
- al   usual   _____, _____
- ish   foolish   _____, _____
- y   crazy   _____, _____
- ary   scary   _____, _____
- ic   heroic   _____, _____
- ble, ible, able incredible   _____, _____
- ive, tive   passive   _____, _____
- ant, ent   dependent   _____, _____
- ing, ed   interesting   _____, _____
- ous, ious   religious   _____, _____
- ate   ornate   _____, _____

WORD FORM EXERCISE

Fill in the missing part of speech:

NOUN	VERB	ADJECTIVE	PERSON WHO...
_____	create	_____	_____
symbol	_____	_____	XXXXX
_____	_____	communicative	_____
art	XXXXX	_____	_____
_____	predict	_____	_____
_____	execute	_____	_____
correspondence	_____	_____	_____
_____	_____	suspicious	_____
therapy	XXXXX	_____	_____
_____	analyze	_____	analyst
diagnosis	_____	_____	_____
_____	_____	educational	_____
manipulation	_____	_____	_____
_____	XXXXX	_____	scientist
development	_____	_____	_____
_____	compete	_____	_____
_____	_____	XXXXX	immigrant
_____	popularize	_____	XXXXX

WORD ORDER IN SENTENCES
If you learn some basic English word order patterns, you will be able to recognize if a word is not in the correct form.
- ACTION VERBS (AV) are followed by NOUNS (N) and ADVERBS (ADV), but never ADJECTIVES

I ran quickly.
  AV ADV

I eat breakfast in the morning.
  AV   N   The direct object (breakfast) should always come RIGHT AFTER the AV.

DON'T SAY: I eat in the morning breakfast.

- LINKING VERBS (LV): be, seem, appear, become, etc. are followed by NOUNS and ADJECTIVES (ADJ)

She is a doctor. LV + N
She appears intelligent. LV + ADJ

- ADJECTIVES come before NOUNS

I read a good book.

- ADVERBS OF INTENSITY (answering the question HOW?) come before ADJECTIVES

I read a very good book.

- ADVERBS OF MANNER (answering the question HOW?) can come after ACTON VERBS

She swims gracefully.

- And ADVERBS OF FREQUENCY (answering the question HOW OFTEN?) can come before ACTION VERBS

She never repeats the instructions.

PARALLELISM EXERCISES
Exercise I

Make the following sentences parallel. In some cases, there may be more than one correct answer.

1. The apartment was beautiful, expensive, and had a lot of space.

2. If you're going to use this recipe, you'll need a pepper, onion, and tomato.

3. Our teacher is interesting: she plays piano, write poetry, and is a painter of watercolors.

4. I always have and always will sing in the shower.

5. Please turn down the television , or will you go to sleep?

6. Michael hopes his dedication, ability, and that he is considerate will help him get the job.

7. Daniel is a happy child and sleeps soundly.

8. Jodie Foster is a great actress and directs movies well.

9. The books on the top shelf are older than the bottom shelves.

10. At the University of Pennsylvania, morning classes are far more popular than the afternoon.

Exercise II

Complete each of the following sentences by adding words, phrases, or clauses that are parallel to the italicized words. There are many possible answers.

1. I was in favor of either *painting the walls purple* or _____.

2. Matt found what he needed in the desk: *a ruler, a pen*, and _____.

3. The square was crowded with young tourists *studying their guidebooks, eating lunches from backpacks*, and _____.

4. Moving to a new apartment means I'll have to *decide what to keep, what to give away*, and _____.

5. During our coffee break we ate blueberry muffins that were *small* but _____.

6. The hats and coats were piled everywhere: *on the bed, on the chairs*, and even _____.

7. Bonnie knew neither *what to say in her letter of application* nor _____.

8. The government will either *ban smoking in public buildings* or _____.

9. Molly walked *across the square* and _____.

10. In the morning newspaper I read *that plans for a second airport are being considered* and _____.

Exercise III

Correct student errors from TOEFL essays, making the sentences parallel.

1. Life is more simple and people are more convenient than people who lived in the past.

2. I think neither spending time with one or two friends nor a large number of friends is preferable to being alone.

3. Some people say it is easy to get into but difficult to graduate U.S. colleges or universities.

4. If the community would be bigger, it would be more comfortable and convenience.

5. A teacher can tell you what wrong is or which better way is.

6. I like to visit a lot of different foreign countries and spending my time with the people there.

7. It helps people to get rid of something they don't want instead of throwing it away but give it to someone who needs and wants it.

8. I don't have to worry if the goods are both damaged or not worth anything.

9. The boss either must decide to hire new employees or retrain the current ones.

10. The unemployment figures for those under twenty-five in Manila is larger than Singapore.

Exercise IV.

Make the following sentences parallel. In some cases, there may be more than one correct answer.

1. After a day at the beach, the children came home tired, sunburned, and hunger.

2.   Larry Bird was a quick, skillful, and energy basketball player.

3.   A good writer edits her work slowly, careful, and regular.

4.   The English composition course contains short stories, a novel, and poetic.

5.   When you write an essay, you should check each verb for agree, tense, and form.

6.   The airline allows passengers to take one, two or third suitcases.

7.   My mother has been a waitress, a secretary, and taught school.

8.   My uncle spoke in a humorous way and with kindness.

9.   I am hot, dirty, and need something to drink.

10. The flavor of the strawberry yogurt is better than the peach.

Exercise V.

Make the following sentences parallel. In some cases, there may be more than one correct answer.

1.   We want to have a flower garden, but we don't know where to begin, how to proceed, or the flowers we should plant.

2.   The summer of 1950 was as hot, if not hotter than any other in the last century.

3.   I neither know what kind of computer he uses of where he bought it.

4.   I am afraid and excited about taking the TOEFL.

5.   Jared has sent resumes both to graphic design firms in Taipei and Hong Kong.

6.   Chris is an affectionate husband, a dutiful son, and kind to his kids.

7.   The shape of the rock, how long it is, and the color reminds me of a small elephant.

8.   He danced gracefully, rhythmically, and with ease.

9.   Judy is a gifted woman: a biologist, does carpentry, and she can cook.

10. Your job consists of arranging the books, cataloging the new arrivals, and brochures have to be alphabetized.

3. PUNCTUATION

Although punctuation is NOT specifically tested in the structure section, it's a good idea to know some basic punctuation rules for your essay writing because if there are too many errors, the readers will have a negative reaction.

1. Never begin a sentence or a new line with a punctuation mark.

2. COMMA (,) RULES

- Do not use commas (,) between two sentences (see run-on sentence section).

- Use commas before coordinating conjunctions (for, and, nor, but, or, yet, so) if there is a subject and a verb before the CC and after it.
    For example: I like black and wear black clothes a lot.
    I like black, and I wear black clothes a lot.
- If you have three adjectives, verbs, or nouns in a row, separate them with commas.
    For example: I like black, brown, and turquoise.

- Transitional adverbs (however, therefore, consequently etc.) have a semicolon (;) before them and a comma after them if there is a subject and a verb before and after the TA.

For example: I   like   black; therefore, I   wear it a lot.
              Subject *Verb*   *Subject*   *Verb*
Also correct: I   like   black; I,   therefore, wear it a lot.
              Subject *Verb*   *Subject*   *Verb*

- If an adjective clause comes after a person's name, you can set it off with commas. These clauses are called nonessential clauses. By using commas, the reader knows the information is NOT essential to the meaning of the sentence.
For example: Jeff Brown, who lives next door to me, works in my office.
              The man who lives next door to me works in my office.
In the second sentence I do not know who the man is, so I don't use commas. In the first the adjective clause is EXTRA information about Jeff Brown.

If I put commas in this sentence   *Students, who arrived on time, can leave early.* It would be incorrect. I don't mean ALL students, I mean *only those who arrived on time*, so I cannot use commas. The sentence should have no punctuation *Students who arrived on time can leave early.*

- Use commas to set off introductory adverbial clauses. If the clause is NOT at the beginning, don't use a comma.
For example: Because I was sick, I stayed home.
              I stayed home because I was sick.

3. Write out numbers. Don't write 10 and 6. If a number is in the millions, you can use numbers. You can also write years in numbers.
For example: Only ten pages of the 6,790,500 pages I wrote in 1992 remain.

4. Use a colon only after a complete sentence.
For example: I took many things to the beach: a blanket, suntan lotion, and lunch.

5. CAPITALIZE the first word in a sentence and the following proper nouns:
- People (*Thomas, President Brown*)
- Places (*Singapore, The Panama Canal, The Empire State Building*)
- Months (*May*)
- Days (*Sunday*)
- Holidays (*Hanukkah, Ramadan, Valentine's Day*)
- Languages/Nationalities (*Swahili, Swedish, Americans*)

Example: Justin visited Doree at the Hilton Hotel in Capetown last Friday, April 5.

Punctuation Exercise

Insert the necessary punctuation. If the sentence is correct, write C.

1. Although Yutaka was absent she e-mailed me for the homework.

2. There are three sections on the TOEFL exam listening structure and reading.

3. I improved my writing ability because I write 2 essays a day.

4. I got autographs from my three favorite movie stars Meryl Streep Jodie Foster and Robin Williams.

5. Jean-Claude has taken several English classes therefore he is confident about his writing ability.

6. Luis Carlos a Mexican didn't want to take a class with 7 other Mexicans.

7. Maria Paula who comes from Colombia explained in her essay why she prefers to live in a dorm.

8. Carmen's daughter was sick so Carmen took her to the doctor.

9. I've been teaching for thirty-two years but have never had a student from Laos or Mali before this semester.

10. Faisal was worried about the midterm and thought about it during the break.

11.   After Diana came to one class she never appeared again.

12.   Luis speaks several languages Portuguese Spanish English and Italian.

13.   I arrived on time for the test I however forgot my passport.

14.   Classes which meet on Monday evenings will meet an additional time during exam week.

15.   !Bravo! If I call your name you passed the entrance examination.

C.   STUDENT ESSAYS

In this section, you will find authentic essays written by non-native English speakers. They are in their original form; nothing has been corrected, added, or deleted. The purpose of this section is for you to get a sense of what a 0, 1, 2, 3, 4, or 5 essay can look like. Two official readers read each essay. In the Answer Key are an official score for each essay, comments from the official scoring guide that explain each score, and *comments in italics by the author.*

- Read the essays one topic at a time.
- Order them from worst to best.
- Decide which score you would give each essay, based on the ETS scoring guide. There may be several of the same score in each topic.
- Compare your scores with the readers' scores (in the Answer Key), paying attention to the criteria comments.
- Remember, scoring is NOT an exact science, but these essays have been scored by more than one official essay scorer.
- For added practice, correct what you can on the essays, paying attention to grammar, spelling, organization, sentence structure, and overall clarity.

TOPIC 1

Some people prefer to spend time with one or two close friends. Others choose to spend time with a large number of friends. Compare the advantages of each choice. Which of these two ways of spending time do you prefer? Use specific reasons to support your answer.

#1/A

Each of these ways are pretty good.

If you spend time with a large number of friends probably you will get more fun and learn out something new from them and so on.

But I prefer to spend time with several close friends. We know and understand each other, have the same interests, feelings.

When I am with my close friends I feel more comfortable and more freely than with a large company.

This is my first experience to study abroad.

In my opinion it is very difficult to mane a lot of friends. For me it takes a long time usualy.

Maybe it's because of we have different mind or I am not active. Also my English is not good. I can't explaine all my thoughts.

So I really miss my close friends in my country.

#1/B

Some people prefer to spend time with one or two close friends. Other choose to spend time a large number of friends. Through my personal experience, I think both of them are fine. Sometimes, I may want to spend time with a group of friends. Sometimes, I feel that I want to be alone or just with one or two friends. I think spending time with either one or two friends or a large number of friends is fine.

I always like to celebrate my birthday with a large number of my friends. I think it's fine to celebrate my birthday, which only once a year, with a group of my friends. I like to share my happiness in this special day. In my birthday, I don't like to be alone or just with one or two of my close friends. I always had fun in my birthday party. Beside, if I involved many friends. I could get a lot of gift too. Therefore, I always have big birthday party.

However, sometimes I would like just be with one or two of my friends rather than a large number of friends. Being with one or two of my friends, I can tell them my secret. When I was in high school, I always went to one of my close friend's house and spent my weekend over there. We always laid on her bed and shared each other's secret. At that time, the bed and the time were just belone to two of us. We didn't want to let anyone else join with us. I think it was sweet to being with one or two friends.

I thin no matter who you're being with or how many people you're being together, the most important thing is to have FUN! You can celebrate something special with a large number of friends. Sometimes it's also sweet to being one or two friends.

#1/C

Some people prefer to spend time with one or two close friends, but others prefer to spend time with a large number of friends. I prefer to spend time with a small number of close friends because of two following reasons.

One of the two reasons is that it is easy to decide where to go. For example, if I go out with ten friends who are not so close to me, I may not know where they want to go because I am not so familiar with them, and because it's a large amount of people, their preference may not be same. But if I go out with one or two close friends, each person knows each preferance and our favorite may be same, because we are close friends. It's easy to decide where to go.

The other reason is that the conversation will be easy and interesting if I go out with one or two close friends. For example, a conversation with a large number of people would be difficult, because ten people, for example, have ten opinions or thoughts, it's going to be very hard to think all of their opinions or thoughts. But, on the other hand, if it's a small number of people, the conversation between us will be very easy and interesting, because each person has his or her friends' basic informations. I don't have to start conversation from the beginning such as "what do you like to do?" or "Which kind of movie do you like?" but I am able to ask or know deep thinking of my friends. To know basic informations about them makes the chat easy, and to know deep feeling or idea is very interesting.

In summery, I prefer to spend time with one or two close friends, because it's easy to decide where to go and the conversations is very interesting.

#1/D

Spending time is an important and necessary issue to think about nowadays. As time is a priceless asset in our lifes; we have to plan how to spend or invest time, especially when we decide to share and spend that time involving other people.

If we decide to spend time with friends, what the best choice could be, maybe spend time with one or two close friends or with a large number of friends.

Spending time with one or two close friends, it could be the best choice when you like to make stronger friendships. The fewer quantity of time you have, the best quality of attention you like to give; then it is easy to organize a meeting with two friends and keep a deep conversation with them than trying to do the same with a large group of friends.

Spending time with a large number of friends is good since diversity of people offer a diversity of characters and personalities, which give you more alternatives of enjoying free activities. A large number of friends is great to enjoy excursions or discover new places.

After said the advantages of one or other choice and having the personal experience as example, I prefer to spend time with one or two close friends than with a large number of friends. Usually, I like to enjoy activities that do not involve a lot of time in preparing it then it is easy to commit one or two people. In addition it is easier to find restaurant tables, tickets, etc for three people than for big group.

#1/F

Some people spend time with one or two close friends, and others spend time with a large number of friends.

Spending time with one or two close friends makes indeed friends. They can speak each other a lot of times, so they can know each other well. It makes strong believe each other. Therefore, They are going to become a real friend.

Spending time with a large number of friends gives you a lot of different experiences. People is not same each other, so you can have many kinds of experience when you meet many kind of people. I am sure what kinds of experience you have, but it helps you when you meet a new person.

Both ways of spending time with friends are good, but I prefer to spend time with one or two close friends because I want to get a real friend.

#1/G

The time in our life and we decide how to spend it, and in the end the time in our days and years, so some people spend the time with one or two others spend it with a large number of friends, any way in my opinion is better, these what I will discuse through this easy.

In my opinion spend time with a large number of friends is better for many reasons. First, with a large number of friends, there are different personality, and these will give varity in the time and will change from hour to onther. Second, when you are with a large number of friends. You can do many activities together, like going in a trip, playing soccur, make a big team to any kind of sports, or make a party. also, with a large number of friends you will find different experiences and different happits, so these as I think will give chance to do and know different things with this group.

Let me give an example when I was in the first year university, I used to be always with two of my friends, and we used to spend alot of time toghther and to go to every place toghther. Do you think I was happy that time? yes. I was happy because there was less argument where we could go, or what could we talk about it, and I knew my friends very well and so they did.

and we could easily understood each other and did the best thing for every body, in addition we couldn't spend more time waiting or staying so really in that time I could do many activities with them. but after a year and a half I was with alarge number of friends and gradually I understood how much love, experiences, different personality, more knolwedge and more injoyable time with a large number of good friends.

#1/H

Friendship is an extremely important component in one's life. Spending time with either two friends or a large number of friends have their advantages as well as their disadvantages. There are different opinions of how many friends one should have and how much happier one would be depending on the amount of friends they have. However, I feel that it is more important to have two close friends rather than a large, foreign group of friends.

Spending time with a large number of friends has its advantages. There is more of a chance that you will actually do something with each other because you have more than two people to rely on. This means that if one person cannot spend time with you, you can always ask someone else. Also, spending time with a larger group opens up your mind to many new ideas and fun activities. There is more of a chance to have diversity in a larger group of friends, where you can learn about different cultures and perspectives. Another advantage is that to the outside world, you can appear happier because it looks as if you are surrounded by many loving friends. It makes people envy you because they think that you are happier than they are. However, this is not the only type of friendship you may have.

Having two close friends has its advantages, as well, which I believe benefit me more than having a large group of friends. Having a smaller amount of friends, I feel, is better because these are people you can always rely on for your personal 55ilemmas. They may not always be able to go watch a move with you, but they will always be there to make you feel good about yourself, on the inside. These are the friends that you will hold onto for a very long time, and sometimes, for your entire life. Having a small amount of close friends means deeper conversations and more one on one activities, where you can discover who you really are and learn to be comfortable with yourself. Having a few, close friends means a lot more bonding time where you can become a part of another person and they can become a part of you.

To conclude, spending time in either a large group of friends or a small group of close friends both have their advantages. However, I believe that spending time with a group of small, close friends is more beneficial to one's self than spending time with a large group of foreign people. Large groups leave you insatiable and craving a relationship, while smaller, closer friendships are undeviating and fill a gap in our lives.

#1/1

Should spare time be spent with many people or a few people? There are advantages and disadvantages to both. In a smaller environment, friendships are closer and in a large environment, friendships are not usually as close. But does this make it better to have a few very close friends than many close friends? Although a friendship may be closer in a smaller environment, the ideal environment is one that is larger.

There are many good reasons why spending time with smaller and closer friendships are good. For example, each person in these close-knit friendships knows the other extremely well. He knows the others likes and dislike. He knows the friend's personal history and knows the times that his friend has suffered or had fun. When there are fights in these close-knit friendships, the fights usually end quickly without bad things happening. It is easier to forgive and forget with someone who has been one of your best friends than someone who has not been as best a friend.

However, there is more fun to be had in a large group of friends. Usually in larger settings, it is nearly impossible to run out of things to do. Nearly everyone has an idea. Also in larger environments, games which take more people are enjoyable. It is more fun to play a basketball game with five on each team than it is to play a basketball game with a few players on each team. Games like capture the flag and such, can be played better with more friends. Video games are also fun to play with many people than a few people. Tournaments can be made and enjoyed with many people. There is also more diversity in a larger setting. It is possible to learn about other faiths and religions. In the end, the ideal setting is a larger one.

1/J   It's good for us to have a large circle of friends. Different kinds of friends make one's life more miscillaneous. In other words, you may have different experience and views of lives. Moreover, when you spend time among a lot of friends, it helps to form a unique leadership spirit. However, I prefer to spend time with one or two close friends for several reasons.

First of all, I feel being neglected sometimes when I are among a large number of people. It's natural that it won't be possible to satisfy everyone's interests in those occasions. Unfortunately, I'm always among the "mute minorities". But when you are with only a few number of friends, this kinds of circumstance never happens, simply because two or three share the same interest. Thus, we all may enjoy our time better.

Another reason is that when I'm among a large circle of people, it's too noisy. One can do nothing but to chat with each other and laugh loud. This is not the only thing that I want to do with friends.

When I'm with only a small number of friends, I can change my mind with them and learn something special. For instance, I learned some details about renascaince in Europe from a roommate of mine when I was a freshman in my university and read some books You'll never have such a good mood to talk about it when you are among a large circle of noisy and garrulous crowd. Also, this kind of interaction helps both of my friends and are gain a broader view of life. Thus, there's an old saying in ancient China that "It's better to have only one but a really good friend than to have a large circle of friends who don't know you well."

Let's find a real friend and make it a better place for us to live in.

TOPIC 2

You have the opportunity to visit a foreign country for two weeks. Which country would you like to visit? Use specific reasons and details to explain your choice.

#2/A

If I have the opportunity to visit a foreign country for two weeks, I would have a difficult time to choose only one. I want to visit many places; for example, among them are

France with it's barocco buildings, foggy England, hot Spain. However, now I am in the United States and I suddenly realized that this country can be the right choice for me. Let me explain why. First, I want to travel here; because U.S.A. is very big and policultural country. Many notions mixed here and produced special one, american nation. I think no one country in the world does not give an opportunity to see so many different cultures in one land. It would be interesting to know how people from different countries can communicate with each other, how they can survive in a new place. Second, if I choose the United States, I would have the opportunity to be in different climates and time zones. For example, people can travel by car from East coast of U.S.A. to west and see how the mixed forests can be changed by savannas and mountains.

Third, I think that fact that people in the United States are very friendly can influence on my choice. Americans like to share their experience of live, because the american nation is the nation of immigrants, people visiting american feel themself at home. Even if foreign visitors do not speak a good English, americans can understand them and remain a patience at the same time.

To sum up, I think that U.S.A. is a right choice for me to visit it, because its people, culture, history, geographical environment are very attractive to people. We can get a different experience here!

#2/B

I think that if I have the oportunity to visit a foreign country for two weeks I'll choose Argentina because the politic situation, the second reason is because the language is the same like in my country, and the third reason is because that is a big country with a lot of diferents places to visit.

The first reason that I explain is the politic situation and that's because I'm a lawyer, and in my mayor I've been studing the governments of a lot of countries and how to grownup a bad economic situation. At the same time, now I think that travel around Argentina can be cheaper than before.

The second reason is the language. In Argentina people speak Spanish and I am Spanish, so for me is very easy understand the Argentine people. As important as this reason is that the Argentine people speaks with a very nice voice, similar as if they are sinning all the time.

The third reason, probably the most importan for all the tourist, is that Argentina is a very big country and you can find there a lot of different places like TIERRA DE FUEGO, a very cold place where all is ice and snow. Latter you can visit LA PAMPA, where you can do treeking. Other place really nice is Iguazu Falls, near Brasil. And you can't leave Argentina without visit Buenos Aires, the capital of the country. This city is very big and there you can hear a TANGO song and dance it.

I think that for all this reasons I would like to visit Argentina.

#2/C

If I had the opportunity to visit any country in the world I would probably chose spain, I think that this choice may create a confused reaction with the readers but I will give my reasons from which I made this chose.

First of all I'm going to say that my native country is Venezuela, may be your thinking "So, what does that have to do with wanting to go to Spain." As you know

Venezuela was an Spanish colony, and I think that may be there's a cultural relation between these two nations, may be that trip would help me understand better the way that Venezeulan culture has been formed.

There's a saying in my country that says that "And old parrot never learn's to speak." So to say you are going to be what you've learned in the first stages of life, hence, I think that maybe Venezeula's failures maybe are because the Spaniards didn't lay a solid foundation for our country.

I also enjoy very much architecture and art, so i've heard Spain has very beautiful museums, such as "El museo del Prado", "Museo de Cordoba", where famous paintings are shown. Also Spain has a lot of history in her streets.

One of my main reasons to visit Spain it's because I'm a big soccer fan and right now their leagues is the best of the world, with high quality players and a lot of competiveness between all the teams that perform in this league. So one of my dreams is to see a soccer game there.

Well those are my basic points of wanting to go there, I hope that now you understand my desire.

2/D

I would like to go to Italy because there are very beautiful, historical and fashionable country. Specially, Italy has very famous of food.

I like Italy but I have never been there. However I know Italy very well because I read many books and watched TV about Italy. I am interesting three things at Italy. Firstly, It is about fashion. Many famous brand companies are in Italy. For example,

Armani, Prada, Gucci, and etc are. They are world wide companies and are making very nice clothes for women and men. Secondly, It is about food. Italian food is very famous around the world. For example pizza, lizotto, vine, hum and etc. They are very nice foods specially. French cooking is very famous in the world. However, the roots is Italian food. Italian king brought these foods to France. Finally, It is history. There are many historical places. Italy has north and south of part. North part has Filenze. South part has Rome and Napoli. Each part has very different cultures and caractors. However, both parts have very historical places also.

I would like to go to Italy. They are very fun to me. I can see and feel good in Italy. There is the best country for me.

Score: 3
An accumulation of errors in sentence structure and usage.
Too many sentences aren't grammatically correct; overly simplistic sentence structure

2/E

I would like visit Japan because it's an amazing country. It's culture is one of the most interesting around the world taking into account that even though Japanese people have a millenary culture and traditions, they a very opend minded about new productions methods and new forms to lead business and finance managements. It is for such reason that Japan is part of the community's countries developed. Thecnological development and the new discoveries that taught place in Japan have made change the world in very important aspects, for example in aspects like communications, transport, finance and computational science, Japan has been a the country leader. But not every thing in Japan is work and studing, one of the most famous international cussine is the Japanese, not only for it's high and exciting quality but for it's beautiful appearance. The qualities of the Japanese Cusine are part of the reach inheritance they have had and so them discipline and serious hard work make part of the Japanese culture.

Other important issue that constitutes a very importan element which makes Japan be one of the most attractive place in the world is its amazing architecture, the forms, color, textures of the traditionals buildingn makes an incredible but beautiful contrast with its modern buildings and perfectly describes the transition of the Japanese culture to the modern world with an interesting and valuable traditionar architecture.

2/F

I would like to go to England. I like England very much because it was beautiful city. I want to go another city in London. I have roommate who from England. I am getting more and more attract about England.

If I go to England for two weeks. Frist one week, I stay in London. I go to see musium, and go to sightseeing, and shopping, and after them I go to another city around London. Probably I can speak English easily and fun.

2/G

I would like visit Japan contry because, I think is the contry most interesting by the culture, the tradition, it's very different then mine, but the principal reason is the people, I have a very goods friends (of course Japanise friends) who teach me what kind of person are they.

I'm interesting in the evolution of that people because the lives in islend terretori and they have a lot of sources, for exaple they have rice, and very important industry, they are the best of the world in electronic industry, othe reason why I want go to Japan is structure of the contry, the houses streets the beuty of all construction.

In education way, I want learn the Japanise lenguage because I think that the future language same the English and I want learn to my major "Internatiol Commerce" and I know if I learn that two principal language, I gonna make a lot business and of course a lot of money.

I think when come true all my dream I gonna make happy and one of my principal drems is visit the "Gans Japan".

In two weeks I can make too many things in Japan, I know I can't learn Japaenisse or make business if I can know the people and know the culture at the same their tradition, and the principal is make come true one of my drems.

2/H

If finance and time permit me to choose a favorite country to visit, my choice will surely be Italy although the communication is a big problem because of the difficult to learn italian. Three points encourage me to make a decision like that. They're following.

The first one is my strong admire to Italian soccer team. As a devout fan of Italy, I'm keeping the belif that Italy will win the champion when world cup comes every four years. Therefore, I hope to live see the series A of Italian soccer league to feel the sense of the true Italian soccer.

Then, the second one is supposed to be the beautiful natural scene in Italy. Someone ever told me that the most charming beach can be enjoyed in South Italy. More, I myself read some books and watched some introductions in TV which all tell the

Italian nature scene as well as Italian long history. Ruins of Roma Empire and the holly church are full of attractive matters.

After that, it comes out my last point to support my trip to Italy. Italy is another country comparing with China, United States and Singapore. Italy has a long history unlike US and Singapore, as well as it's developed unlike China. The trip to Italy should be a very different experience for me. I'm looking forward to more by expericing difference from my familiar environment, because of my adventrous personality.

Frankly speaking, I've planned to travel throughout the world including the Africa, Antarctica. But Italy'll be my first stop during my rest of the global trip.

2/I

If I have a change to visit a foreign country for 2 weeks, I will choose USA. Because there are a lot to see in USA, and the transportation is very convenient, so that you can travel to a lot of places within 2 weeks.

As a country with a large landscape, America has all kinds of sceneries to see. You can see white snow and ice in Alaska, enjoy the sunshine on the beach in Florida, and experience the Great Canyon in Colorado. Actually, you can experience all four seasons within 2 weeks in the lovely country.

On the other hand, America is the most developed country in the world. You can see a large variety of high-tech products and enjoy all kinds of high value-added services during your stay. Moreover, you can have some touch with a lot of cultures and races for US is an immigrated country.

Last but not least, America has a highly developed transportation system. You can reach every corner of the US by train, by bus or by plane and the fares are usually reasonable. Usually you can reach your destination safe and sound without being exhausted so that you can enjoy your trip.

A lot of us have US dreams, deam to see the Statue of Liberty, the White house, etc. So why not go to the US for traveling if you have 2 weeks time?

2/J

If I get a chance to visit a foreign country for 2 weeks, I would like to go to India. India is always my dream land. It has a long history and colorful culture just like my country. It is so mysterious and wonderful. It attracts thousands and hundreds people like me from all over the world every year.

The begining of my knowledge about India is from those wonderful folk stories which my parents told me when I was still a child. Those colorful folklores reflect its colorful history and culture. From then on, my dream about India starts.

When I grew up, the more I knew about India, the more attractive I found it. There are many kinds of religions in India and it's the birthplace of Hinduism. So it is also a country of religions. You can find people with different religions live together harmonly. It will surely be interesting.

As I'm a person who want to experience different cultures by interacting with the local people, I wish to have a chance to see how people live with my own eyes and interact with them to feel their culture with my heart.

Although I have known a lot about India by books and TV, there are still pretty more interesting things about this old country waiting for me to explore when I get to this wonderful land.

TOPIC 3

Some people think that they can learn better by themselves than with a teacher. Others think that it is always better to have a teacher. Which do you prefer? Use specific reasons to develop your essay.

#3/A

I think it's always better to have a teacher. Maybe some people think that they can learn better by themself than with a teacher. However, if they have any question, there is no one can teach them.

There are many reasons that make me to think it's always better to have a teacher than studying by myself. For example, if I'm tring to solve a math problem, and I have no idea how to answer it. If there is a teacher, the teacher will tell me how to solve it in many ways. And the next time when I meet same kinds of question, I'll know how to do it. However, if I rather study by myself, I may never know the anwser. Maybe I can find the book in order to help me, but the book will just me the anwser. I won't know how to solve the same kind of question.

A teacher also can tell you if you're doing wrong. Sometimes you don't even know when you're making a mistake. People always make some mistakes, but they don't want to keep making same mistakes again and again. If you're learn boxing, it's always better if there is a teacher with you. The teacher will teach you if you're in wrong posture, or using wrong hand. It's very important to know whether you're right when you are doing sport, because any wrong posture many injure you.

A teacher can always teach you something and you can always keep asking question. After someone teachs you enough knowledge, you have to study and remember by yourself. A teacher can tell you what wrong is, or which better way is, but if you don't study, nobody can help you. Therefore, I think having a teacher is always better than studying by yourself. However, whether to learn or not is totally be descide by yourself.

#3/B

Besides parents, teachers are the most important people in our life. We have "Teacher" this word since long time ago. It must have reasons why the teachers exist in our socity.

If people just study by themself, they hard to solve the problems. When people study alone, they will always use the same way to think. They might have same problems again and again, but they will not notice that is wrong. If there is a teacher, he can see different point with you.

When the teacher beside us, he can watch us to make sure we are no lazy. For example, when I was in junior high school, almost every student study in school. I told my self, I can study by myself. So, I went home. However, I never studied, I just watched TV, and I fail the text.

No matter what you think. Teacher play a important role in each one's life.

#3/C

Regardless of gender, age, religion, and nationality, teacher's role in learning is enormous because a teacher is a guide who will help open my eyes to some specific field which is totally unknown to the student. Also, in broad meaning, old civilizations like

Greek, Rome, Egypt and China, and different cultures from mine has been good teachers to the human being to achieve today's civilization.

First, imagine a society without school. That society may not have difficulties in food, housing and clothing which are most essential facts for survival, but it's impossible to expect civilization there. Teacher's role in school is to help students to shorten time for them to achieve the goal in life.

Secondly, there's a saying that nature is teacher. Not only geographically but also periodically different cultures provide human being good materials to learn. Nevertheless, it doesn't mean students don't need teachers. Only if teacher, student and good materials are harmonized, good learning conditions are available.

As a result, when students want to learn something, trying not to emphasize one fact only is essential. Harmony between student and teacher will provide the best condition.

#3/D

I prefer to have a teacher because if I just learn by myself maybe when I do or I learn something it mistrake. Sometime when I have problems. I can't find it out, how i can do it but if I have a good teachers, they can help me and maybe they can find out my problems and improve me to something it better. But if I just wait for my teacher help, I thing, I can't improve my English language and TOEFL too much. That mean if I want to develop my English very well I want to help and learn by myself too. How I can develop very well? I think, it isn't just study in classroom and read books at home. I want to parktice listening and speaking by talking to many people, listening radios, watching TV or movies. How you can talk to other people if you just know grammar but can't use it to talk and

#3/E

When people learn, they must know how to study most efficiently. There are so many various people, so some people need teacher, and others are not.

In my case, I prefer to student following teacher's lectures. After taking lecture, I always review by myself.

I cannot study by myself. Also, I cannot belive why some people prefer to study alone. The question is remaining my head, so I will try to figure out against this problem.

This following is made hypothesis.

First of all, some people, they want to learn without teachers, have not ever met good teachers. They are so selfish that they could not adjust with their teacher's tempo. Secondary,

#3/F

Some people think that they can learn better by themselves than with a teacher, others disagree. I prefer to learn through experience, because I think that you can only learn by yourself.

In drivers education, a teacher lecture for 36 hours about driving, laws, and safety. I did not pay attention at all in the class, and I am a good driver; I am the only person I know that got a 100 percent on their drive test. My peers in drivers ed often paid more attention than me, but still did not get great scores on their drive tests. This is because they waisted time trying to learn from a teacher, I learned to drive by myself.

Throughout school, one has many teachers. Most are bad, and often not too smart. Since the first grade, I have had two good teachers. I think that I have learned alot; I can read, write, think, debate, and articulate my ideas. I did not learn this from my teachers; but on my own. In fourth grade, I had a despotic and moronic teacher who shall remain nameless. She used to punish me for reading in class. She didn't teach me, I had to teach myself, and she was upset and abusive because she knew that she couldn't help me.

The above two examples illustrate how people learn individually. They don't need the help of a teacher, just the will to accomplish on their own.

3/G

The learning process may be stimulated by the presence of a teacher or by the self motivation of the student. This short paper will attempt to examine which way is preferable.

Learning with a teacher enables the student to have a structural environment. The teacher will determine the curriculum, the lesson plan and the homework. One needs only to follow the teacher and perform the work to benefit and learn the subject matter. The structure is also extended to the timing of the learning process. Classes are held at specific times and specific homework is assigned. This enables the student to methodically build his grasp of the subject.

Learning by one's self is not as structured and is dependent to a large extent on the motivation and self decipline of the student, the material studied, the time it is studied and the pace is entirely up to the student.

While studying with a teacher may seem more efficient, it may deprive the student of creative thinking and flexibility. Having to be in class at a certain time may be burdensome.

On the other hand, studying by one's self can lead to lack of regiment, slacking and motivation. I would personally prefer some kind of combination and integration of the two methods. A limited roll of the teacher, more as a facilitator and motivator, coupled with a large degree of flexibility afforded to the student, will be my preferred method.

3/H

Some people think that they can learn better by themselves than with a teacher. Others think that it is always better to have a teacher. Which do you prefer? Use specific reasons to develop your essay.

3/I

Regarding the ways of learning, everyone may has different point of view. Some people think they can learn better by themselves while the others think that have a teacher is better. I've come to my own conclusion. There are three reasons that I think learning with a teacher is better than by myself.

First reason is efficiency. Since the teachers have organized the informations that want to teach you, you can get the point more easily and quickly than learning by yourself. The second reason is interaction. While learning with a teacher, you can ask him/her to explain the parts that you can't understand immediately, and can discuss the questions or doubts you have. It's better than learning by yourself without others' help.

Most important of all, you can get some treasures that you can't find in the books from teachers. In my opinion, the most valuable things are not only the knowledges in the books, but also the ways that other people thinking, especially the ones who have more experiences than you. Besides, you may also get some new ideas when you interact with your teachers.

The reasons above show that's why I prefer to learn with a teacher than by myself. Although some people may have different point of view and disagree this, nevertheless, I think the reasons I've said are persuadable.

3/J

It's true that one could not learn sth. very well without some important instructions from teacher. Teacher can often unwrap your puzzles, give you new idea, different ways to try out. However, it's also sufficiently imperative for all of us to culture the custom of learning by ourself. The is as follows"

First, one should spend enough independent time reviewing what he or she has learned, trying to figure out what's the proplems and how to solve it. I mean one should first think over the problem before asking teacher.

Second, Innovation should be very necessary part of the whole study framework. One should not follow exactly as what the teacher tell you. If we do so, the whole society may not progress any more. So we often look up the interesting things in the library, do the same problem from different angles and try to make a breakthrough on the former basis, etc.

Finally, different people have different ways of thinking. We may often be confused by teacher or someone else, although there is merely easy proplem. In that case, we must insist on what we think and try to "translate" the alien things into our own.

As I said previously, we also need help from our teachers, So we should be open but close. It's always possible that we may plunge ourself into the puzzleness and do not know what's wrong. Then, we can refer to teacher to seek for solution. Your teacher may see clearly what's the crucial points as he or she judges it in a general view.

In total, to my opion, it's better to combine two methods together and use it wisely. It's complementary to each other and should not be apart from each other, neglect one or the other. We also shall emphasize one but the other depending on different occasions. Only when we grasp the spirit of this organic integration can we do more better in life.

TOPIC 4

In the future, students may have the choice of studying at home by using technology such as computers or studying at traditional schools. Which would you prefer? Use reasons and specific details to explain your choice.

#4/A

I have been thinking about studying at home by using technology such as computers or television long time ago. If students can study at their home instead of going to school, they can study more comfortably.

At first, people can study with their computer screen, speaker microphone at home. They can also record something such as lectures, documents and whenever they want to review, they can use with their computer.

In my case, I took a lot of classes on internet.

Although it was not standard course, I felt comfort a lot.

Secondly, the more time is gone, the more students going to attend school. But my country is very small and environment for education is bad. If they can study at their home. We don't have to worry about those problems.

On the other hand, this way has some problems too. If people study at home, not only they can't make friends, but they will feel boring.

Lastly, people who want to study at home can study very easily because their computer has dictionary, calculator, encyclopedia, and so on.

I'm a student still now, but I also wish that a day which I can study at home easily will come as soon as possible.

For these reasons, I prefer studying at home by using technology than studying at traditional schools.

#4/B

Studying at home by using technology or studying at traditional school

In the present time, it is quite natural that students go to school to study. In the future, however; the system of studying at school will change completely; student may have choice of studying at home by using computer or television or of studying at traditional schools. If I assume that I'm a student in the future, I'm sure I'll choose studying at schools, even though I sometimes feel lazy to go to school.

Why do I choose studying at schools? Through my experiences as a student, I know it teachs us a lot of things; not only studying subject such as, English, history or math, but also society's rule and people's relationship. For example, if students go to school and attend the class, they will see many friends and teachers. Those students will enjoy having conversation with their friends. If teachers or friends have different opinions from them, they will be upset about that. However, those students will realize there are several kinds of people in the world and each person has each opinion.

On the other hand, if they don't have to go to school, they will have nobody to communicate with in addition to their family. Probably, it is very easy that they don't need to go to school, but when they have questions and need help, who does help? Even if computers or televisions can teach them, I can't imagine studying without my classmates, because studying with someone such as, teachers and classmates have helped me in several things. Sometimes, they encourage me, sometimes they comment on me and give me directions.

Therefore, I'm sure studying at schools gives students many things, and I believe experiences of studying at school will be unforgettable for students.

#4/C

Students have many choices of studying way in future. Basie on technology improve everyday. More knowledge we have to know. In my opinion, I bias to computers.

Undoubtly, each style of education has good side. But if students chose television. Maybe almost of them watch "funny show" or entertainment program instead. They couldn't be able to concentrate on their work. If chose traditional education. They must learn many subjects before that they never interested in. Even though unrelative with their occupation in future.

"Computer," it is a very important tool and we have to learn to operate. I can get more information from it. A lot of species I in the wide range. And it is very fast. In this society is focus on efficient. First come, first served. So I chose computer.

#4/D

I would like to prefer traditional school because if all of students chose computer or television to study, they can't make relationship. I think this is very big problem because, if you do not have relation ship you can't do everything and your maind is getting why, I think most of society is made by good relationship. And second reason, they will be getting fatter because they will stay at home almost one day, and they helth is getting bad, because they do not go out to play or something to do. When I was junior high school student, I always stayed at home to play video game and then I was getting fatter. And third reason, if all of student chose the way to study; then don't necessary teacher, may be most of teacher lost the job. If they lost the job, they can't get the money and who can't live any more so

#4/E

The introduction of communication technology may one day change the way we view schools. Staying at home connected to the internet or viewing courses on TV may render today's schools obsolete or force them to adopt to new realities.

This short papers will examine the choices confronting a student when selecting a traditional school versus one that uses technology that enables remote studying.

Information desseminatet via the internet can be presented in an more efficient way. Teachers and students can be more focused on the subject rather than in a classroom environment. On the other hand, the personal interaction between teacher and student and among students makes the discussion richer.

Cost of tuition can be a major factor. Traditional school, with its physical facility and staff is most likely more costly to run than one that uses remote studying.

Traditional school is more than just a conduit of information. Social life which is a major part of the traditional school is almost non existant in remote studying.

Studying on line can enable the student to have more flexible schedule than the rigid schedule at a traditional school. This may enable students to hold a job which they may not be able otherwise.

In conclusion, the adoption of a new technology can be incorporated into the structure of tradional schools. I would prefer to see traditional school using new technologies to make them more cost effective, more attuned to the individual needs of the students while, at the same time maintaining the vibrancy of the social interaction which make them an exciting place to be a part of.

#4F

I agree that students have the choice of studying at home by using technology such as something because for example. A man is sick now and he can't go to school. He can't study, but if he uses technology such as something, he can study. He may not go to school. Now. We can use Internet around the world. We can do something by Internet. The Information Technology improve every day. I think that Information Technology is useful. Two reasons. One is we can use it easy and if you know something we know almost to use Internet. The other is we use Internet.

#4/G

It is possible in the future that students may have the choice of studying at home. Their teachers will be the technology such as computers and TVs etc. But would it be a good choice for them? There are several reasons why I don't prefer studying at home.

First, we learn more than educational things in school. School is not just an education unit, it's more like a society. There are teachers classmates and rules in school. We learn How to behave and how to live with people, and also how to cooperate with others.

Second, Education is the matter of communication. But with the teachers like computers? It's an advanced way to communicate but still I don't think it's the best way. Exchange emotions and thoughts things like that are more important that knowledge itself

Last, it's a little bit of combination of these two things that I have mentioned, studying at home alone is not helpful to make a well-around person. We need to belong the society which we called school and we also need to communicate with people alive.

Studying at home and studying at school both has negative and positive sides. But no matter how the technology is getting into our lives deeply education should be remain as the field of human being and I don't want to lost the benefits that I can have from shooling

#4/H "Why Be Social?"

At schools, children learn many things. Grammar, math, and science are all pressed upon a student throughout their school days. However, there are other elements of school that cannot be taught in the classroom. By going to school, children interact and become friends. If school was run at home by televisions and computers, then children would miss out on an outstanding social opportunity.

People need to interact. It is part of our nature. As a child, I mostly interacted at school. I made friends, we talked, and we got to know each other on better terms. By going to school, students not only learn to read and write, but they also learn from their peers about how to treat others. Without the social aspect of school, there would be no reason to stop hitting the snooze button.

In the future, children may be able to be educated by their televisions and computers. There are two problems with this. The first one is variety. All of the teaching programs would be the same and there would be no place for arguing or debating with the program. This aspect ties into the second problem, the lack of interaction. Students would not be able to communicate with, teachers, administrators, or fellow peers. They would be forced to interact with a computer program.

Spinoza once said, "Man cannot survive in solitary confinement." Having a program teach a student lessons is exactly that. There are no other children around to interact with. These programs may help our education but they will take away our ability to socialize with others.

4/1

What's the purpose of school? Some people may say that school is the place to get knowledge, learn many different types of subjects. But many people also say that school is the place to make many friends. Which idea would you prefer?

When my mother was young, she was a teacher at kindergarten. Her students were often wrote letters to her about their primary school life. Many letters said that they got many friends at school and they were having exciting activities such as excursions. I also enjoyed such activities when I was in primary school. I visited famous parks, car factory, bread factory, museums. I am sure that all students enjoyed them.

Today's school style is changing now. Students can get education at their home without going school. Using computers and internet, sometimes phone too. I think this system is very useful for some students who live very far away from school. If students need 5 hours to get school that would be serious problems. And also transportation is big issue too. If they can't get any public transportation to go to school how can they get school? For those reasons I think this system is not bad. But would recommend it to you child? I guess that many parents say no. What's the reason? The reason is clear, they can't make friends.

For the first day of school how did you feel? Were you nervous? Worrying about making friends? Those experiences are very important when you become adult. When you work. And other thing is many special experiences from school. School offer many experiences for students, those may bring big interest for students. Maybe students think as their work after school.

I think school's main purpose is make many friends and get many experiences with other students. For all reasons I prefer to go to school.

4/J

The opinion of the students may have the choice of studying at home by using technology such as computers or television or of studying at traditional schools is all alright, but it still depends on the person who wants to study, what they are going to study, and what is the purpose of the study itself.

I, if I am asked to choose, I think before I decide what my preference is. I would like to share you about my opinion since the three ways of studying have their own advantages and disadvantages. Firstly, studying by computers, nobody says that it is bad, but this kind of thing less human because we only see or get the knowledge from the packed material. Everything is already set up and we only sit, listen, and do the assigment. Indeed, we can have internet access, but still, if we are unclear about the material, we cannot ask directly eventhough we are allowed to ask the question exactly at that time, but, we seldom get the answer directly. And more, after one problem there can be the next and soon, and yet, we need the answer at that time.

Secondly, studying by television is similar to computer. There is a little bit difference: by computer, we can have on-line access but by television, it is merely a boring time. We are really treated like robots. We are merely asked to sit and listen and take a note. It is really not gorgeous way of studying. At the mean time, waiting for meeting teacher or the expert directly is really takes time eventhough sometimes this kind of thing offers us to ask questions or explanations directly by phone, but the problem is we have to race with other audiences too to have a chance for getting the answers or explanations of what we have asked.

Thirdly, studying at traditional schools is also not too bad. Perhaps we should limit the term of "traditional" here. Is it traditional in teaching method? for example; the way of teachers teaching is translation method? Of in terms of facility? Well, if we assume that it is limited on the facility, it means that the school doesn't have computer lab, language lab, or other sophisticated facility like internet. I think it is okay since the teachers are well educated, well trained, and good performance. These all things are more important that the electrical equipment because it is friendly and we can ask questions directly.

So, finally, I would like to say that studying by traditional schools is better because I like to communicate directly with the resource person and more friendly. And also I can discuss what subject should I take and what is the right choice for me. I think these all things are better by asking directly to the teachers like what traditional schools do.

TOPIC 5

Is it better for children to grow up in the countryside than in a big city? Do you agree or disagree? Use specific reasons and examples to develop your essay.

#5/A

I prefer childern grow up in the countryside than in a big city. I would like to explain the reasons: Firstable, there's a place on your own where peaceful is great. As a second point, the nature has the answers for everything and it's marvellous to love it. As a last point, the creativity will be higher than if you're in a big city.

I'm trying to explain more widely: Peaceful, love and creativity are three key points to think where's the best place for children grow up.

I suggest another way: live in a big city and go on weekends to the countryside. This mix can be useful because children will have two perspectives: the life in a big city and the life in the countryside. They have to study in the city and at the same time they learn from the nature.

In past, I've seen the results in some kids and it works.

#5/B

Children are better to grow up in the countryside than in a big city. There are a lot of concerns for a child to grow up in a big city. A big city usually have large population and serious pollutions. If I have a child, I wouldn't bear him/her in a big city but the countryside.

The environment in the countryside is usually better in a big city. My family and I lived in a big city three years ago. The noise, the air pollution and the crowd made us very uncomfortable. My older sister always had problems with her breathing because the terrible air there. In terms of living in a big city, people couldn't own the space as big as they need. A lot of people have to either rent a place or live in a tiny apartment. My family decided to move because they want to give us better environment and larger space to enjoy ourselves.

We love to live in the countryside. You won't always feel a lot of people are around you. There are no pollution in the countryside. The river, the air, and the whole environment are extremely clean. It's the best place for living. If I were a child, I would like to live in the countryside. I would like to be beared in the place where has less pollution and noise. I would like to see clean river and enjoy large spaces.

#5/C

Many people might disagree, but I think it is better for children to grow up in the countryside than in a big city.

One of reason is that children learn many things from nature. For example, in summer they can go swimming in the sea and meet many fishes; while they can go to mountain and find plants and animals. They can learn many things by themselves. Second reason is that there are a few people, so they do not feel to stress out too much. In big city, children always have to compete to another children, so I think they stress out too much.

In big city, chirldren always have to compete to another children, so I think they stress out too much, while children who live in countryside do not compete many times. They can study with their friends and help each other.

Third reason is that countryside children have many times to talk their parents. I think to live city is so expensive. That is why their parents work until night, so their children eat dinner alone. Eventually, they can not learn from their parents. For example, social rules, mannars, greeting and habits. Countryside children can learn from their parents about them. Forth reason is that I grew up in country side, and then I feel it is right for me to grow up there. Because I am a person who can feel nature beautifully, who helps another people and who knows social rules. I think, thanks to my parents I can grow up this kind of person. They gave me many styles of education.

Finally, I think it is better for children to grow up in the country side than in a big city. To live in country side is good for their education. Children can study not only their school, but also nature.

#5/D

I agree with children to grow up in the countryside. I grow up in the countryside. My hometown in country. It is very beautiful place. This place has around mountain, and nice sinery. I think that children grow up place is better than town. When I was child, I always play in the beautiful 85atures with my brother. Now I remember for nice experience. I think country side is better, however I consider about children's education that big city is better than countryside. Countryside has a little schools. So big city has many schools. Children where live big city almost study very hard, becaus big city has many schools, and we can chose schools. The child getting more and more interested in about study. When I was high school student. My hometown had only one university. We have to go Tokyo, or we have to go this university. It is no choise.

My hometown's children not interested in about study. I think education is very important for children. Children have to study very hard.

If I have a child, I hope that I want to live countryside and grow up my child, because I like nature very much and when I was child, I grew up in countryside, I think where it nice place for children education.

I agree with this topic.

#5/E

It is better for children to grow up in the countryside. There are three reasons about that.
First, there are many mountains in the countryside. Recently a lot of children are poor at sight so mountan's green color helps them from poor sights. Also in the city many people suffer from air pollutions. If children live in the countryside, they are much healthier than they live I the city.
Secondly, They can play outside in the countryside. They have enough space to play with their friends. If they do that, they can explore the nature. Thirdly, they can be optimistic in the country side. There are a lot of stressful things in the city. If they live in the country,

Above all I was grown up in the countryside. It was very helpful for me to live there. Children need the nature when they are growing up. That is why it is good for children to grown up in the countryside.

#5/F

As you walk down a street you feel the true experience of life all around you. There are huge skyscrappers covering the city, in which the sun reflects off of. The air is filled with noise pollution of honking cars and talkative people. This is what life should be like. Living in a big city is better for children to grow up in, rather than a countryside because of the wisdom they will learn, the atmosphere.

The wisdom a children will learn from growing up in a city, is one that could never be replaced. When one grows up in a city you get to learn about all different things. Small countryside areas tend to keep thing quiet, and secret, where as a big city is real and straight forward. Living in a big city myself I would never stop being greatful for the gift of knowledge I received.

The atomsphere of a big city is a great experience for someone to grow up in. A city up bigging is a lot about the streets and survival. The skills you gain, in a big city, you can use everywhere. If you can survive, in a city then you can survive anywhere. You learn to deal with traffic, subways, fast cars – everything. If someone from a countryside came into a city, they would be confussed. However, a city person would be able to make it in a countryside.

In conclusion, city life is the best. It helps to develop someone as a person and to grow up faster, thus becoming more mature. A country up bringing will not provide a children with the tools he or she will need to "make it" in the real world.

5/G

I agree that it is better for children to grow up in the countryside. Because there are much opportunities to see another people who lives in the same area.

For example many parents who live in countryside pay attention for the children even if the children were not their children. While some parents who life in a big city doesn't care any children.

And again I think the children should touch nature, animals and plants. There exist a lot of nature in countryside. But the children who live in a big city can't touch nature so much times.

Off course There are some disadvantages in countryside, For example the problem of education.

Totally I agree that It is better for children to grow up in the countrysind than in a big city.

5/H

I do agree that it is better for children to grow up in the contryside than in a big city.

Now, in a big city is very noise and populated while enroviment in countryside very frest and quieit. If children live in countryside, they can play outside in helthy enroviment, So it is good for their helth. In fact, children live in the countryside are often stronger than children live in a big city.

People live in countryside more friendly than people live in a big city, So it influence children personality, So children live in countryside often have good personality.

Many

5/I

In my opinion, it's better for children to grow up in a big city, instead of countryside. There're many reasons for me to think so. And here I'll present some of them to you.

First, generally speaking, big cities have better education system than countryside. I can give you a example. In my hometown, a small countryside, there're only one school primary. After graduation, students have to transfer to other places for further education. What's more, the education quality there is not very high because of the poor hardware quality.

Second, countryside always don't have enough hospitals that are very important for the health of children. My childhood was spent in countryside. Each time I was ill, I had to big cities for a cure.

Third, the children in big cities have more clourful life. Because there're a lot of facilities in big cities, children can go to zoom weekend, visit museum in holiday, watch movies in night, and so on. I think such things are very important for the growth of children.

In addition there's still a lot of things playing a crucial important role in children's life in big cities.

So, I think that it's better for children to grow up in a big city.

5/J

As the global economis increased this century, more and more people lived in the cities. A lot of people sugested that it's better for children to grow up in the countryside than big city. I agree with their opinion.

Firstly the children living in the big city will have chance to contact the high technology. There are lots of science museum and technical labs in the big city. They can go to the museum frequently to learn about the laws of nature and improve themselves. Some of them will be interested in science and become scientists in the future. If the children grow up in the countryside it's not easy for them to be close to the technology and develop a deep understanding in science.

Secondly, the life in countryside is quite simple and you know only a few persons even after you live in countryside for years. The children living in the countryside seldom learn about what happen around the world and have few chance to learn the new thing. One the other hand, the children growing up in big city have to face different kinds of people everyday and know more about the world. During the communication with the others, they can learn how to handle the life, how to get on well with all kinds of people and how to solve the problem they meet. And the children growing up in the countryside have to learn those things after they come to the big city. Their paces will be slower.

In conclusion, it's better for children to grow up in the big city than the countryside. They will know more and perform better.

TOPIC 6

Some people believe that college or university education should be available to all students. Others believe that higher education should be available only to good students. Discuss these views. Which view do you agree with? Why?

#6/A

Even though colleges or universities education in the US is comparatively available to all sorts of students rather than Japan, some people believe that higher education should be available only to good students. However, I don't understand why those people think so because I strongly agree with system that gives all students opportunity to get higher education rather than that of Japan.

Through my experience, I realized US colleges and universities have a lot of advantages to all students. Most schools in the US don't have very difficult entrance examination, but they require all students to study hard to graduate. Having easy requirement gives students many chances. For example, it is possible that the students who used to be not good students in their high school probably will be interested their study in their college or university students life. In addition, requiring hard work makes students being responsibility because if they don't study hard, they cannot graduate easily. Therefore, Japanese people say it is easy to get into, but it is difficult to graduate from US colleges or universities.

If the US higher education is available only to good students, some students won't have chance to get higher education. It is because they may will require students high grade in order to get just good students.

In conclusion, American higher educartion system gives our students alot of chance to study, and also it makes us strong and responsible because our grade and graduation depend on how much we study hard. I believe those students who used to have several opportunity to study and study hard will make good future.

#6/B

College or University education should be available to all students. In many countries the education is an economical and politicoil problem. Only a minimal part of population have access to universities or colleges, because the tuition is high. Many people cannot study because they don't have enough money to pay the tuition.

In this direction, I agree with education should be available to everybody. In academic item, the competition is stronger.

Only the best students will finish every program.

It isn't necessary to do that difference, because the academic system have the solution. This way, to higher education arrive the best students from all program and from all countries.

#6/C

I agree with the view which is that university education should be available to all students.

First, I can't understand what is good student. Does good student have a lot of many, a lot of knowledge or kindness or everything? I can't understand this point. I want to be revealed it.

Next, for example, if there is the man who is poor, dosen't study hard and, but, he is geonias, should university education accept him. My opinion is yes. because it is high percentage that he gave benefits for society or world. I think it is failed that the person who have good talent of some part isn't accepted by society.

Society is constructed in the many kind of persons. We shouldn't refuse the person who is not much the society.

#6/D

I believe that higher education should be available only to good student. But there is one problem that what type of students are good or not.

For example, almost student never study before semester's exam after entering University or College in Japan. They just want degree to enter some good company. But They had good score at high school.

While there are some student's who couldn't get good score at high scool study hard at University or College.

Finally, when the judge of entering to University or College can be done correctly, I agree with the opinion which higher education should be available only to good student.

#6/E "Joining in Real Life."

You have to work if you wanna be succesful in life. If you wanna be a doctor, you have to study human's body. You can not sit all your life and be a doctor. You have to go to high school, university then if you want to be more sure about your job you go to master.

University is a place where you seperate from your childhood and start to do decisions about your future. You choose your job, you learn how to do it, you work so that you can learn better. In these days people can not find a good job if they do not go to university.

I believe that every student have to go to college. It doesn't matter if a student is good or not. A student can not like chemistry or biology and won't be a good student but he or she can be succesful in college. High school and college are very different things.

In university you have more responsibility. You are alone, without your parents try to learn stuff so that you can be someone in future. Universities can accept students by their succes but it doesn't mean that bad student can not go to university.

If they accept only good students to college what happens to the other. You become an adult in university. You start to do your works, you take responsibility. University is a place where you join in real life. I do not think only good students can have this choice.

#6/F

Going to college is a very important stage in one's life. Some believe college should be available to only good students. However, I believe every person deserves the right to learn.

The top schools in the US such as, Harvard and Princeton are well known. Success in such schools requires very knowledgeable person. An unintelligent person may not be able to succeed in such a place, therefore a good school, especially in the Ivy league should only accept top of the line students.

Throughout the US there are many cheap public colleges. These colleges should accept all aplicants and when there is no more room there they should refer people to a different school. Everyone deserves a proper college education.

In the final analysis colleges should be open to all. It's not right to allow a person from having a full education. Everyone deserves the choice whether to go to college or not to.

#6/G

College or university education must be available to all students. There is no reason that only the good students have a chance to further their education. Most poor students need another chance to succeed in school. They need guidance. There is also an argument to the other side. People believe that students should be rewarded for their hard work while the other students should, in a sense, be punished. They believe that if the good students are put into an environment with other good students, they will all strive to the best, in turn helping them succeed.

Many poor students have not been guided correctly. They should not be punished for something they could not neccesarily handle. Most of these students just need another chance. Depriving them of a college or university education will only cause them to feel negative about themselves. Instead of being in school, these children will be in the streets getting into trouble. Since they have no other way to support themselves, they may possibly get involved with selling and buying drugs. These students must not be given up on. They must have a chance.

On the other hand, some people think the good students should be rewarded by giving only them a chance to have a good education. However, these people are wrong. These students can still be given a college education even if the poor students also have this opportunity. Why can't both groups of students have a university education available to them? Hence, while the good students should be rewarded for all their hard work, the poor students, too, should be given a chance to succeed in life.

6/H

I think that college or university education should be available only to good students because it is important for them to keep quality of education and to have will which student want to study.

First, I think that college or university education should be available only to good students. If all students come to college or university, their quality of education would fall down. For example, Medical school and dental school are needed high level students because these have a lot of responsibility to grow good doctors.

6/I

The availability of college education, to the better students or to all students (who say, graduate from high school) is controvertial. This short essay will examine the pros and cons and will attempt to reach a conclusion.

1) Resource allocation – making higher education available for the better students will allocate scarce resources more efficiently. The investment in higher education will be utilized more efficiently by the better students. College education for poorer students may become an inefficient resource allocation. On the other hand, larger school as a result of more universal education will operate more efficiently at the micro, or individual school level due to economies of scale.

2) Raising the skill level of society – college education raises the skill level of the individual as well as the society in general. However, the better students will likely benefit more than the poorer one since higher education may be more suitable to higher level. A less academic student may benefit more by attending a vocational school. Society may benefit more if education is matched to the academic level of the student.

3) Personal advancement – In a society which emphasizes college education the lack of one may be detrimental to the personal advancement of the individual.

Lacking college degree may not give equal chance to various member of society.

In conclusion, higher education may open the door to all to advance in life. The availability of college education will make society more democratic as it will afford more equal opportunity to all. Despite the possible misallocation of resources the overall level of society will rise as more members are afforded college education, and hence, the benefit to society will far outweigh the additional cost to society.

6/J 1

In these years, there is an argument about high education. Some people said all students in high schools should receive high education, say, in universities or colleges. But others disagreed with them. They said only the qualified students should get so.

In my opinion, I refer to the latter one. From the point of a biologist, everyone is not born the same with others. From another point of one social scientist, the background of each student is also different. So, these two factors determine someone would be good at researching, someone be good at hand-working, someone be good at sporting. That's just the need of a society which must arrange different groups of people at different positions.

In contrast, if we put all students no matter about someone are qualified or not into universities or colleges, what would be the result. To lower the level of textbooks, some excellent students would be common or be wasted just for the reason to make all students pass. To keep the same level as current level, lots of students would not get their diplomas. That's also a waste of time for them.

So, from the above two points, I think the exams for entrance into universities or colleges are necessary to ensure some qualified students would get their qualities in researching, art, and so on fully developed. The other students would find their favorite positions in the other fields. It's one good distribution of human power, I think.

TOPIC 7

Some people believe that the best way of learning about life is by listening to the advice of family and friends. Other people believe that the best way of learning about life is through personal experience. Which do you think is preferable? Use specific examples to support your preference.

#7/A

Some people believe that the best way of learning about life is by listening to advice of family and friends. Other people believe that the best way of learning about life is through personal experience. In my personal opinion, I think the best way of learning about life is combine the advice from your family and friends, and your personal experience.

When you take the advice from your family or friend, you can let youself never make same mistake as your family or your friend has made before. However, what happen to you or the situation may be totally different that what happened to your family or friends. Therefore, listening to the advice or family and friends is not enough for learning about life.

In your personal experience, you can always remember what you have done. You can remember how you made the mistake, and at the next time you won't made same kind of mistake again. However, when you're learning by yourself and never take the advice from your family and friends, you may need to spend some more time or money to make something done.

I think both of them have strong poing and shortcoming. If you can combine these two two together to learn about life, that will be

#7/B

When you Have to decide to choose one option about what it is the best way learing about life some people think about advice from other people. Other learn about life from their own experience, However I prefer to Have both options.

First of all. It is very Important to me that everyone, who knows perfectly about something, about live can give me an advice. For example when I was a child my mother told me so many times that I could not cook without adult supervisd because I would burned or something like that, well once I was cooking to myself. When I saw Fire in the kitchen. Nobody was at home, so I Had to call my Uncle who lived near to my House. Fortunally Nothing happened.

Second. Living your own experience is very important too. Something's you can not learn From other people. You Just have to live to learn. For example When I was 20 I began a relationship, with a person, who was, Jelous, selfish, and other kind of faults. I remember all of my Friends, who were worrying about the situation. They said to me that I Had to leave that guy. However I did not realize that they were right until. I felt in Jail myselft. Then I decided to broke with him

In conclusion, I can see for my personal experience that sometimes is Good. Listening people who know about, but others not.

#7/C

Each person think differace that they way for a some information.

We get many informations from TV, newspaper, book, listening and expierence.

I think that the best way is expierence.

I think the importentest is expierence. For me

But by the expierence, I got a little.

Because, My expierence has a limit.

So I get more by second way.

For example, They are TV, newspaper, book and listening

Although I get more information by second way, the expierence is more important for me.

For example, about one thing: many people have each opinion

They are a little bit difference.

It's difference about thinking for themselves.

I cann't get every opinions. If I get every opinionce that I will complex.

And I believe my expierance.

Sometimes that is wrong.

First I will choose by my expierance.

If I don't have expierance about it.

Second I will choose by second ways.

#7/D

Human being has become skillful person by listening many things from his family or friends or by learning through his personal experiences. I believe that it is useful that they become skillful person through their own personal experiences.

First of all, before I played tennis I had watched a lot of tennis match at courts and on TV. I believed that I could play tennis as good as a mature players who played very easily ways. And I went tennis court and began to play, but I could not hit the ball well. Then I realized that people could not do anything. Through their personal experiences such as training. It was not good for playing tennis that I had a lot of tennis knowledges.

Second of all, human being don't image their situation without their experiences. For example, I planned to go to US for studying English but I couldn't get image that I was in the U.S.

In conclusion, personal experiences are necessary for knowing everything which are useful for good living. Of course family and friends teaching are also important but people should get their skills by their personal experiences.

#7/E

Listening to people's advice to learn about life is beneficial, but is not effective unless the listener is able to experience what has become common knowledge on his own, and to incorporate other people's views, through these experiences, into his own philosophies. A symbiotic relationship, thus exists. A person who has been told everything all his life, but has never gone out on his own, will be completely foreign to the responsibilities necessary for self-reliance. In my situation, experience is more preferable.

I have been lectured all my life about being responsible and being careful of my possessions. I always lose things, nevertheless. It is experience that I need to finally begin to stop losing things, especially if I need them. I lost my calculator once, then borrowed one from the school, then lost that one, then got one from my friend. Since I wasn't faced with the problem of not owning a calculator, I never came to realize how much I needed one. My grandma yelled at me everytime I've lost something, but she never left me out in the cold without a calculator. I came to Brandeis Summer Odyssey and I lost my watch because I put it in a safe place and forgot about where I put it. I panicked so much because I needed the watch to know when classes started or when freetime was. Finding the watch in a safe place made me happy that I had known to keep it safe.

Back home I wasn't forced to do any chores like make the bed, but here I have to do them myself because otherwise I will live sloppily. I had to learn how to do the laundry because at home my grandma always yelled at me to do the laundry, but she'd do it for me anyway. She would teach me how to do it time and time again, but I never did it, so I kept forgetting. It is hard to forget how to do things if you have to do them, though.

Listening to people's stories are amazing and sometimes inspiring, but if it has no relevance to my life I cannot make my life into someone elses. People's success stories in how they achieved their dream cannot make me achieve my dream of playing basketball professionally. I have to take it upon myself to practice and work toward my dream. I have to overcome my own hardships, and find my own inner light. Yesterday I didn't play so well at basketball and it was because I was having a bad day. I need to find out how to make my game better, hence my day better.

I am inclined to believe that though both are neccessary factors in people's lives, experiencing moments are much more effective lessons than simply hearing advice on how to live. One could not live without experience, locked up in a cave, hearing stories, because he will have never lived his own life. The best way for a person to get to know himself is to learn through his own experiences.

7/F

"Around the Circle"

I'm seventeen years old, and I don't believe that I have learned about life by myself. That's because I'm a stranger on the world, trie to learn about life by listening people's advices or opinions. But I believe that after a certain time, when my parent won't be around, I will learn about life through my personal experience which is the best way.

My parents are my guardians. They don't want to be hurt by someone or something, however I'm aware that my parent won't be around one day. I'll be all by myself in this world. That'll be the time when I learn the life through my experiences. I will suffer the consequences, or sometimes be awarded. That will depend on me. I'll choose the Right or wrong. I will choose my own way where I will be happy. I Remember when I was a child, my father tells me not touch the oven, but I always sneak out of the Room and go to the kitchen. I was curious why oven is dangerous. And one day, my father let me touch the oven. Since that day, I understood that oven I dangerous which burns my hand. When I look back I know that inside of my mind I listen every word of my parents, Because they know the Right. But this way is preferable when your parents are around you.

As you grow, your opinions change very month or even every week. I'm going to be considered as an adult in two years and my parents or my friends are still giving me advices. That's fine with me, but in some ways, I want to be free. I love my family or friends and I respect them. I listen and consider every word they tell me. My parents know better than me, because they experience the same situations before and know what's the correct way to deal with it. My friends also experience before unless they won't give me advices. I'm getting matured and I can see that listening the advices help me to get along with the problems.

This is like a circle. You start experiencing through your life and you give advices to your friend. Now I'm in a stage that I take advices and also learn about life through my personal experiences. I believe that I will be in a stage that I'll give advices depends on my personal experiences.

7/G

I think that the best way of learning about life is by listening to the advice of family and friends.

First, You can save money to go to school. If I want to learn it by myself, I need to study it in a school. If you ask your family or friends, it will be free for you. If you want to collect an information of learning about life alone, you need people who inform you. When you want to do it without any helping from people, you should have a burden. Finally, It's the best way to learn about life.

7/H

I think the best way of learning about life is through personal experience. We have each our own values, so nobody understand other person's lives. Similarly, the way of learning about life is various for me, so we can only know the best way by each person.

Certainly if we can use the best way of learning abut life, we may find the answer than we exactly want to. We can touch the different values, experience of their own. In addition, this way is indirectly as safe.

However, the life is our own things. The responsibility of our life is depended by ourthelves. It is impossible for us not to suit for their values totally. It is important to recognize what is the best way of learning about life is the necessary in our life. Challenging and directing to know the best way is the first step of our way.

7/I

How many times did you heare advices in your life? and How many timed did you make a good things or a bad things and learn from these bad or good things? to answer these questions, let me discuss what is the best way of learning in the life by listening to the advice of family and friends or from person experiences?

In my opinion the best way of learning in the life is through personal life, for many reasons and I will give my personal reasons. First, the advices can be forgotten quickly, How many advices we heard through our lives. And how many advices still in our minds, I think a few of them. In the other hand the mistakes which we have did it, impossible to forgetten.

Because it is like traces in our days, mind and in deep experience. The people don't like to repete their mistakes or bad things because the felt the pain and tried the bad reaction for their fault so they learned by this way better than the advice.

Second, we we lesson to the advice we use only hearing, but in experiences all the tens like feeling, hearing, testing, thinking, touching and seeing are used, So the lesson will be strong and deep. As Aristo (Greek saintest) said "teach me, I will forget, but share me I will remember." for an example always my father advice me to be care when I'm driving my car, and he repet this advice every morning but I didn't be carful until I made an accident and me let was broken.

Third, The experience give the person chance to expiere his knowledge in different way. When you deal with people you discover different personalities, and you lern how to communicate with. let me give you these example, last month new employee came to our company he has strang personality, calm, silent and almost seem sad. Nobody could communicate with him or unless talk with him. But I could because I had wide experience in personalities, my friend told me she heared many advices about communication, but non of them help in this case. Also onther friend said, "I read 20 books about the personalities and that didn't help me, you experiences are the best"

In conclusion, advices are being heared, experiences are being learned, and every body use the Advice and the experince to paint a new life to herself or his self.

7/J

Enjoying life during learning about life is most people's opinion to life. how can we learn about life? Some people believe that the best way it by listening to the advice of family and friends, while others prefer to learning through personal experience. My life tells me that the later is my favorite. The followings are some of my explanations.

Personal experience can give me a real view about life. When I try my best to know what life is by my own behaviors, I have to do a lot of things. Some times I suceed and sometimes I fail. Just during different successes and faliurs, I know what life is. Comparing with friend's advice, maybe some are even faults because of their good hearts, I prefer to learning about life by my own way.

Further more, personal experience can encourage me to fight for my goal. Someone once said, happiness exists during the process while not only at the end. I believe it. So I can not wait for others' advice during executing my plan. I do everything what I could to get near my goal and reach it at last. That I like to learning about life does not mean I neglect others' advice. Some good advice can help me avoiding many mistakes and to get success quickly.

In my opinion, enjoying life is the most important no matter the methods you use. So my advice about learning about life is try your best to feel, observe and execute your life.

TOPIC 8

The government has announced that it plans to build a new university. Some people think that your community would be a good place to locate the university. Compare the advantages and disadvantages of establishing a new university in your community. Use specific details in your discussion.

#8/A

Advantages and disadvantages of establishing new university

Establishing new university in my community will influence us many thing: both positive and negative thing. Some people may agree with that plan, others may not. Many reausons can be good point and at the same time, many facts can be bad point.

In my opinion, the plan of establishing new university in my community is good thing and I agree, even though I found some negative effect to our community after building new university. Because if new university would be established, it gives us a lot of positive things such as, community's growth and more opportunity to get higher education.

For preparation of finishing building university, our community need to develop everal things such as, city, institution and equipment in order to welcome the coming students. Our community should be great srounding for students, because those students' academic experience will be important for their near future. I believe these development will be positive influence for not only students but also citizens. If the community wold be more big, we will feel more convenience and many young people will feel they want to stay their hometown, these effect's related to make our community more enegetic.

On the contrary, some people may think making our community bigger because of establishing new university is not always good thing. After completion of building university, the population of our community will be grown and city will be more crowded then now. It my cause rising price, difficulty of finding place to live and environmental issues.

However, I still believe establishing new university brings us more good thing than bad things, because development of community makes citizens being like our sroundings and give great deal of experience, although those citizens don't go to outside.

#8/B

For a long time, my community has wanted the government to establish a new university in our city. Establishing a new university in our has some advantages and disadvantages.

One of the advantages in about the economy of the community. When a new university is established, because many new people, students, will come to study, their economic demand will increase economic activity and revenues of business and people in my community. Also, because new student will come to my community, people living in my community may interact these new people, and social relations may increase.

Besides its some advantages, establishing a new university in my community has some disadvantages. For one thing, in our city rents are already high. When new people come to community, rents will become higher. Secandly, in our city, roads are not enough under present circumtances, so traffic jam will be increase when a new university is established.

To conclude, establishing a new university in my community has some advantages and disadvantages. I think it is a good idea because nothing in the world has exact advantages without disadvantages.

#8/C

The university is the higher educational level. For this reason, in order to stablish a new one, the government has to look about some important features of the community to get the highest benefits.

In my community there are two education institutions of high level, which offer many different and attractive programs: one of them is public and the other one is private.

But, on the other hand, my community has a high rate of growing. The group of teenagers is very large a most of them are enrolled in the high school programs. Furthermore, there are three big factories which workers, young people, are interested in to improve their educational level.

In conclusion, the government and the community has to study and look for the best solution for the educational development of this population.

#8/D

There are several advantages as well as disadvantages to building a new university in my community. Building a university requires an immense amount of vast area. As a result, space must be found in my growing community. In addition, with a university, there are many new jobs, which may benefit people in my community who are currently searching for jobs. The new university may help the economy amelioriate. There are also many disadvantages that are encountered when building a new university. First of all, the population will rise. Secondly, the citizens in my community will have to pay more taxes.

Building the new university in my community may be beneficial. First of all, students will be encouraged to pursue their dreams by attaining a higher education because the university is close to home. Also, for the students that can't afford to go to the university, funding may be available for them because the university is in their town. Another advantage to my community would be that people may be able to find jobs easily. Due to the fact that my community is in a suburban environment, a number of citizens go to Boston for work. Boston is a half an hour commute, and as a result, many people are looking for jobs closer to home.

On the other hand, there are many disadvantages that come along with building a new university in my community. First of all, the government would require citizens to pay more taxes. Another disadvantage would be that because my community is continuously growing, we would have to stop the multiplying population to make room for the university. However, students who attend the university may live in my community, which would add to the population growth.

In conclusion, there are both disadvantages and advantages to building a new university in my community. Unwealthy students living in my community may be compelled to get a higher education because funds will be provided for them. On the other hand, creating space for the university will be an issue because my community is large and is continuing to grow.

8/E

Ichigaya, it is located in center or Tokyo, is my hometown. There are some good and bad aspects to build a new university there.

First of all, it is located in center of Tokyo where is the capital of Japan. Almost all trains and metros pass this town. That works until midnight every day. However, whoever have to have lots of pain in the morning time because many people use this station.

Last of all, students can enjoy Tokyo very much. There are many theathers so they enjoy their private life. However, that is so expensive. It might be bothered students finances.

8/F

Nowadays, Universities play quite important roles in the world. In fact, the human society can not develop without technology and science. However, to build a new university in a community may cause controversial disputes.

These people in our community who are on the opposite side of building the university will give out the following resons. First of all, they believe the existence of an university will change the lifestyle of the community. Since there are a large number of students and faculty in the university, the community might become crowded and noise. What's more, those who dislike the plan may insist on that the starting period of building an university would be orderless. Many buildings need to be constructed and a lot of facilities should be made. All these disadvantages can bring inconvenience to the people living there.

However, in my opinion, the advantages brought by the existence of an university are of great value. I can give out strong evidences for my point. Since the university is always a place for people to learn knowledge and do research, it will definitely construct a nice environment for the whole community. As a matter of fact, the campus of an university is also very beautiful. People in the community can enjoy their lives there. Those facilites such as swimming pools, sports fields ect. can also be helpful for us to relax there. The most attractive point is that you can study in the university with you own family nearby. It is very convinient for you.

All these advantages given above weigh so heavy that I firmly believe the plan to build a new university will be of great value to our community.

8/G

The Advantage and Disadvantage

Lots of people in my community disagree with the idea of building a university nearby. But, others consider it is a quite good idea. To my point of view, the plan has more advantages than disadvantages.

Firstly, the plan of setting up a university can stimulate the economy in our community, even our whole town. A large amount of investment will flow into this area definitely. Everybody living in our community will benefit from it. Obviously, the university will need lots of employee after it is built up. Therefore, it increase the employment and create new opportunities.

Secondly, the university will own a number of advanced facilities, including library, swimming pool, playground. These will open to us and provide serious entertainment. What's more, the university will attract more and more children to read books. This will decrease the crimes of the children.

However, some opposite will say that the new university harm the environment of our community, since at present our town is a quiet place to live in. But, I really think we can control the noise by more strict law. Also, we can invite the students in our house. Thus, they will live with us together compatibly.

From above points, we should conclude that setting up a new university is a wiser choice.

8/H

I agree to establish a university in my community. Why not? There are so many advantages.

Firstly, University is a place where high technology exists. If it is located in my community, we can learn much more about the new high tech by reading the posters or attending their lectures. As I know, most of the Universities have free lectures. It is quite a great chance to catch up with the trend, isn't it?

Secondly, the students in the University can do much help to us. For example, we can find techers for our children more easily than before. And, we can hire them as part time engineers with relatively lower money. Yes, it's good to them as well because they need work expiriences and extra living expenses.

Thirdly, here comes another reason that the students can help improve our atmosphere by affecting our community. They are active, healthy and positive. We the residences will follow those always existing around us. Yes, the surrounding is very important for the children. I dare say the prospective university will increase the scores of our children inderectly.

Of course, there are also some disadvantages such as it will make the traffic more crowded and so on. But I think we should not worry about it because the government will sure to solve the problem for us.

Totally speaking, I hope the new university will be founded here.

8/1

Recently, the government has announced that it is going to build a university in North Point, my community. Some think that its location to build the university I wonder why

North Point is one of the most crowded places in Hong Kong. How can they come up with a idea of building the proposed university in such a noisy place? One of the most important criteria of a university is it's peaceful and quiet environment whereby students is able to concentrate on their studies. Building a school in North Point is definitely not a wise idea.

Additionally, North Point is a small place and has limited space for building a university. One have to bear in mind that a university is a not short term project. Once it is built, it is going to be there for hundred years or even longer, so we should make sure there is enough space for the extension projects in the future. It would be better if it is location in a newly developed city in the rural part of Hong Kong which provides sufficient land for future use.

The only thing I can tell that is good to build the university in North Point is that it is convenience. It has a good transportation system and located in the middle of Hong Kong. Students will have no problem of getting to the school.

However, it is obvious that the downsides of building the proposed university in North Point overwhelmed it's advantages. By considering more thoroughly and wisely about such a big project which has profound influences on our community. Other better spots should be adopted.

8/J

The recent announcement by the government of its intention to build a new university has created a stir in our community. Some local people believe that the best place for this new university is right here in out midst. This short essay will examine the advantages and disadvantages of such a move.

Access and transportation – while our town is located at a far end of the country, it enjoys excellent network of highways from major population centers of the country. This will enable students, parents and staff easy access. The local transportation, however, is another matter. The daily gridlocks, lack of parking and inadequate local streets will be made worse by the addition of thousand of people and cars.

Prestige and reputation – adding a new university will enhance the prestige and reputation of the community. This, however, will not be of the greatest importance since the area is replete with many highly ranked university.

Adding to the local economy – To the extent that most students will be from outside of the area, the local economy will benefit from the infusion of tuition paying population. This will enhance employment, add to the property values and create the multiple effect by supporting local businesses that will serve the new population. On the other hand, an influx of people will put a strain on the local services and infrastructure, such as water service, police, fire and social services.

The effect on non student population – The arrival of new, mostly young people in large numbers can change the fabric of the community. While, as previously mentioned, the economy may benefit, local residents may resent the aspects of student life, such as loud parties, excessive drinking and careless driving. In conclusion, while the community may benefit to a large extent from a new university, the adverse effect on local life should be carefully evaluated.

TOPIC 9

Do you agree or disagree with the following statement? Children should be required to help with household tasks as soon as they are able to do so. Use specific reasons and examples to support your answer.

#9/A

Teaching children to do household tasks is a training. They must know how to help their families as soon as they are able to do so.

When children can help to do tasks, they will learn that what responsibilities are. Parents give them jobs to do, and they should finish thoes completely. I have helped to wash dishes since I was ten years old. My sister and I did this job together. We knew if we didn't do it well, we had to use dirty dishes. We knew it's important to take a responsibility.

Every child will leave their parents someday. They will live alone or have their own family. They must learn how to do household stasks; however, they can't do those by themselves. I have a friend who lives in the dorm. She never help with household tasks at home because her parents didn't want her to spend more time on homework. Now, she lives with a roommate, and she still can't clean her room. Her roommate does all of the tasks. They don't have good time together because her roommate complains her roommate complains her all the time.

Parents should teach their children to help with household tasks as soon as they are able to do so. A good habit should be given when they are young, so they will keep this habit forever.

#9/B

I think the children should be required to help with household tasks as soon as they are able to do so because parents can give their children to some knowledge and to be found them as a family members.

First, the children should be required to help with household tasks as soon as they are able to do so because parents can give their children to some knowledge. For example, Parents can teach their children to cook some dishes. Children are going to learn how to use knife or how to bake or how to boil something.

Secondly, the children should be required to help with household tasks as soon as they are able to do so because Parents teach children who are the one of the family member. For example, If there were many household tasks, parents should separate and give some work to children. For my experience, when I was in junior high and high school student, I often clean our bathroom and clean the dishes after dinner.

In conclusion, I agree that the children should be required to help with household tasks as soon as they are able to do so because Parents can give education to their children. To work for family. It is good oppotunity for parents to educate children.

#9/C "Children and Household Tasks"

One of the discussions that is going on about raising children in the right way is about whether or not children should be expected to take part in household tasks as soon as they are able to do it. Children should be required to help with the household tasks as soon as they are able to do so since they will learn to take responsibilities, how to live in a community and feel more confident because they can do something useful.

Helping with the household tasks as soon as they are able to do will help children while developing their characters. When a child is required to tidy his/her room, she/he will learn that he/she is responsible for keeping his/her own room tidy and will learn that she/he has to do it in the best way since its her/his responsibility. In addition to that, helping with the household tasks will give the family members the opportunity to do something together and the child will learn how to take part in a community, in his/her family which is the smallest unit of the society. A child who helps her/his mother to prepare the dinner will learn that he/she cannot expect others to do the things that she/her is responsible for. Moreover, tidying a room, helping someone to prepare a meal, or helping his/her parents in the garden will make the child feel and think that he/she can do something useful and a result the child will feel more confident.

As a conclusion, helping with the household tasks will help the development of a child since the child will learn feel more useful, gain self confidence and learn how to live in a society.

#9/D "A Simple Task, A Simple Choice"

Children should be required to assist in household tasks as soon as they are able to do so because of the positive effects which result from working in a community, which they will have to do for the rest of their lives. Simple household tasks benefit the child more than the family in that it takes more time and effort of the parents to teach and nurture responsibility and life skills than it take the child to actually perform the task. Hard work also leads to the appreciation one feels for other people and all they do for you. When the process of accepting work, taking responsibility, and appreciating your own situation begins, then the ideas of sacrifice for the greater good and living in peace start to develop.

Responsibility is nurtured by the authority figure and forced upon a child at first, so eventually the child will realize how much taking responsibility for oneself is beneficial. Life skills such as cooking, cleaning, doing the laundry, taking out the trash, and doing the dishes will help and stay with the child throughout his/her life by becoming accepted as a part of life which is necessary for cleanliness, survival, and efficiency. The appreciation of others, of life, and of work is also encouraged and developed on a strong structure of self-respect which will help the child grow into a compassionate, yet well-rounded person. One choice to have a child take responsibility, develop pride, and work for the common good will always be remembered, appreciated, and lived.

9/E

In china now, lots of families have only one child. So the special educations of the only child in a family become more and more important today. Among them, one big question is should children required to help with household task as soon as they are able to do it? In my opinion, I agree with it. I'll give you three reasons as following.

First of all, house work is good for children's health. In some meanings, Housework is also a kind of exercise. Especially for some light works, like wiping the floor or cleaning the table. They can help children get some exercise at the same time doing housework.

Second and especially important, leave some housework that just belong to the children themselves. It's a good habit for them to do their own things by themselves. They should learn of depending on themselves but not others from their childhood.

Last but not the least, housework makes children consider more of other people. If in a family, not only the mother or the father does the housework, but also the child does it, the child can actually feel how tough and hardworking it is. Later, the child will keep the floor and table clean when he is in home, because he knows it will cost his mother several minutes to clean it. Even more, the child will help his parents to do some housework, when he see them tired. It's really a good character for children to always consider others.

So, that concludes my opinion. I think it's better for children to do some housework which they are able to do, especially for the only child of their family.

9/F

It's necessary that parents let their children help household tasks as soon as the children can do so.

First of all, doing household tasks is very beneficial for the kids themselves. Kids are usually curious about the world and want to try everything so why not give them a chance to try. With those practical work, children can know the outside world more quickly then just being isolated from those simple tasks.

Secondly, while doing housework children need communicate with parents. There comes another chance! Parents can know about their children more, then learn what the kids realy want, what are their preference. If you don't want your child to do anything, you will kill all of the chances to know him. We know a lot of kid are afraid of talking with their parents or unwilling to talk with their parents. This undeniably results from lacking of communication from the beginning. The less the communication, the more unwilling to communicate which leads to less and less understanding between parents and kids.

Thirdly, parents can also benefite a lot beyond understanding your kids! Why don't you think it's perfect that your housework is being reduced with days going on? Your children are growing up and doing more and more housework. One day, you can retire from kitchen! Isn't it a good plan? So try to let your kids do something they are able to do, if you don't like house work!

In conclusion, children doing houseworks can benefite both kids and parents.

9/G

Nowadays, As the living standard of the people's life has been increased dramatically, the average people live a higher quality life, they're often busy on their work, and care a little about their housework. Some of them just hire cleaner for cleaning their house every week. It often happens that parents don't ask their children to do the housework for them, actually the children can do some of the housework. I do think that is a bad thing.

For one reason, and the most important reason supporting my opinion that children should do the housework as soon as they are able to so lies in the fact that housework really can improve their capability to deal with problems they can get a lot of practise and try to do the things in different ways, find out what's the best and most efficient way to solve problems they encountered while doing housework. That really contributed a lot to the children's imagination and creativity in the late days.

Secondly, Doing housework also shape children's character during the period of growth, that train children to be more independent to become people can stand on their own feet and with sense of liability, for example, many people in China only has one child. So they spoiled their children a lot and didn't ask them to do any housework in the home, they treated their children as the center of the whole family, but what happens is that all their efforts and goodwill didn't be rewarded with good results, the children are always relying on their parents to do all the things for them so, when they grow up they will become very dependent on someone else, that's too bad for a person don't has a ability to survive with himself.

Finally, I want to mention is children can really help their parents a lot while doing some housework for them. As we all known, the adults have a lot of work to do in the weekdays, if children can do them favor, that really help them a lot, then the whole family will be more harmonious and happier.

In one word, Doing housework really do a great good to children so children should take the liability to do the housework as soon as they are able to do so.

9/H

I agree that children should be required to help with household tasks as soon as they are able to do so. There are three main reasons why they should do this.

The first reason is that it will make children independent. Independence is very crucial for every one of us. If someone always depends on others, he will achieve nothing in his own life. To help with household tasks teaches children they should do something for themselves, such as cleaning their own room and making fruit salad for themselves. It will be quite helpful to be independent before they leave their parents to fight his own future.

The second reason is that it will make children more responsible and more willing to help others. Children can learn that they should do something not only for themselves, but also for their families and even for the society. Helping their parents with the household tasks, such as washing everyone's dishes and cleaning the kitchen will offer them prize from their parents. Thus, they know that if you help others, what you do will be appreciated.

The third reason is that it will be physically good for children. When children help with household tasks, they get the chance to do some exercises, which will probably make them stronger.

In conclusion, it's not only physical benefits but also mental benefits children will get from helping with household tasks.

9/1

Should children be required to help with household tasks as soon as they are able to do so? Definitely yes, In my opinion. Children should take part in household tasks as nearly as possible. It's very good for children's growth.

Many points can support this opinion. The first of all, children can learn many life-skills for their future life. No matter how young is a kid, he/she will live independently someday. At that time, he/she must do cleaning, laundry and cooking by himself/herself. That means, every child will have to do some household works after he/she chose to live independently. So, why we don't give them opportunities to learn to do it earlier. The earlier they learn to live independently, the earlier they chose to do it. Indepotent is an essential factor for adult person.

Secondly, children can experience cooperation when they do house hold task. Many household work, such as house cleaning, can't be completed by only one person, especially for kids. So, they have to cooperate with others. After a long time of such experience, they will be fit with cooperative work style. Cooperate is the fundament of our society. A child with such factor will tend to help others and be likely to finish his job with others' help. In short, a cooperative kid will become a kindly person.

Finally, sharing the household tasks will let the children know that, working is the basis method to live. In doing household work, kid will know that, no laundry then no clean clothes. So, they will know that it is working that gives them what they need for a happy life. After they grow up, we will meet a group of enterprising youth. From this way, our society can develop forward.

In conclusion, parents should enable kids to do household tasks as soon as they could. It's important not only for the children's growth, but also for the development of our society.

9/J

Children as part of the family members are sometimes required to involve in the household tasks. This phenomena has bring both advantages and disadvantages to not only children themselves but also to our society.

Children should be required to help with household tasks as soon as they are able to do so because they should contribute to the family since they are a part of the family. Household tasks should not falls on the parents of a family only. Children should learn to appreciate the contributions of their parent and thus they should try to help with household tasks.

Besides, children should learn to deal with household tasks as they should be independent in the future. Therefore, this is a great opportunity for them as a starting point to learn with those tasks. Children should be independent and know how to take care of themselves because they are going to leave their family as they grow up.

On the other hands, there are some disadvantages if children are required to help with household tasks. As children are too childish and always careless dealing with household tasks, this might cause accidents to happen and therefore household tasks may be dangerous to children in this care.

In addition, children play an important role in our society children should gain as much as possible knowledge during school period. They should concentrate on their homeworks and not spending most of their time on the household tasks. Children may feel too tired after finished their tasks.

In conclusion, parents as the guide of children should compromise, so that the problem of children involve household tasks will be minimize.

EXERCISE ANSWER KEY

WRITING THE ESSAY
Brainstorming Exercise
Answers will vary.

Thesis Statement Exercise
Answers will vary. Here are some possibilities.
1. Although playing games is fun, it's more fun when your team wins.
2. Because I've always lived in an apartment building, I think it would be more interesting to live in a traditional house for a change.
3. Although some people say zoos have no useful purposes, I've been impressed with how children become more animated when seeing animals.
4. Even though my high school did not require students to study art and music, I wish my high school experience had been more well-rounded.
5. Although I usually listen to music for background noise, I become more relaxed listening to music when I'm feeling bad.
6. Although teenagers may see themselves as adults, it's only when one lives alone that one becomes more of an adult.
7. I might want to build my own home on a piece of land, but I know it would be more beneficial for my community to build a park on that space.

Introduction Exercise
Answers will vary. Here are some possibilities.
1. It doesn't give any specifics.

2. A better introduction, but which games specifically?
3. Too specific to be an introduction.
What makes this introduction different?
More developed, leaves the reader wanting to read on, doesn't get too specific with the details.

Introduction and Thesis Statement Exercise
Answers will vary. Here are some possibilities.
1. We see thousands of advertisements every day: in newspapers, on television, on the Internet, on billboards. Although occasionally I may learn about a product that I don't know about that might improve my life, I sometimes am seduced by advertising to buy things that I don't really need.
2. I live in a technologically advanced country. We no longer rely on animals for farming or transportation as we once did. If I were to choose the most important animal in my country I would select dogs because they provide companionship to so many people that would otherwise be lonely.
3. A building that special meaning to me is the Museum of Fine Arts in Boston, Massachusetts. I grew up in Boston and fondly remember running among the mummies with my visiting cousins and many years later taking my children there for enrichment classes. Today whenever I have time, I steal away for a few hours and revisit familiar treasures and discover new masterpieces.

Combining Agree/Disagree Exercise
Answers will vary. Here are some possibilities.
1. One or two friends: you can know them better, they like the same things you do
A large number of friends: you'll never be bored, you'll talk about many different things
Thesis statement: Although some people enjoy being with a large number of friends who keep them from being bored, I prefer to spend more quality time with one or two friends.
2. All students: some students mature only when they're in college, society needs all of its members to be educated
Good students only: because it's so expensive to educate students, only the good ones deserve it, good students have proven already that they can handle the pressures of college
Thesis statement: Many people in my country contend that only good students should be allowed to attend university; however, I'm convinced that students who didn't do well in high school should be given another chance if they so desire.
3. Outdoors: healthier, chance to interact with nature
Indoors: not polluted, quieter
Thesis statement: Even though some of my friends spend all of their free time on nature walks and camping, I prefer the quiet and tranquility of being indoors.
4. Should do: go beyond comfort zone to experience something new, learn more
Shouldn't do: stressful, life is too short
Thesis statement: I have complained about doing some activities in my life that I don't enjoy; nevertheless, these very activities have enriched my life.
5. By hand: unique, creative
Machine: cheaper, saves time
Thesis statement: Even though the objects I cherish the most in my life-an oil painting done my best friend and a sweater my grandmother knit-are hand-made, I realize that it's

too expensive and too time-consuming to decide that all of my clothes and furniture should be hand-made.

Topic Sentence and Supporting Details Exercise 1
I.
1. TS: A SP: B
2. TS: A SP: B
3. TS: B SP: A
4. TS: A SP: B
5. TS: A SP: B
6. TS: A SP: B
2. TS: B SP: A
3. TS: B SP: A
4. TS: A SP: B
5. TS: A SP: B

II. *Answers will vary. Here are some possibilities.*
1. Young children learn cooperation and other life lessons through playing.
   Young children discover the world through play.
2. Children learn most easily when they're young.
   If children learn study habits while young, they'll always find studying to be easy.

Topic Sentence/Supporting Details Exercise 2
1. A   2. B   3. A   4. B

Transition Exercises
I. *Answers will vary. Here are some possibilities.*
1. I'm one of those persons who loves to be in a large group of friends.
2. I can't think of any benefits that zoos provide to either the animals or the visitors.
3. from the earliest years, teachers and parents should encourage game playing.
4. the teachers can get suggestions of things they could do differently.
5. a shopping center would bring thousands of cars, creating traffic jams and causing pollution.
6. my inability to teach myself.
7. the Earth has no more room for all the items I discard to make room for new purchases.
8. I decided to take the TOEFL test and apply for admission to an American university.
9. I enjoy modern art and music.
10. art and music enhance one's creativity, which can be applied to every field.

II.
1. c.   2. a.   3. a.   4. b.   5. a.

III. *Answers will vary. Here are some possibilities.*
1. ...semester although I....
2. ...homework, whereas my
3. ...buses; moreover, I had.....
4. ...had; hence, I signed.....
5. ...essays; moreover, I'm

Conclusion Exercise
Answers will vary. Here are some possibilities.
1. Although a movie is usually spectacular and engrossing, when I read a book my imagination transports me to another world which I often prefer to watching a film.
2. Whenever I look for a new apartment, I first ask how many rooms the place has.
3. I can think of a dozen countries I would love to visit, but the one at the top of the list is Australia.
4. Some of my friends are satisfied with their lives; others seem to be always searching.
5. The first time I saw the commercial with the Japanese monkey listening to its Sony Walkman, I thought to myself "what a clever designer"!
6. I like my school, the teachers, the curriculum, and my classmates; however, I hate having to wear a uniform.
7. I was surprised to hear that some American students choose what they study, for I believe that experienced educators should make curricular decisions.
8. When I think back to family crises and times of tragedy, our being able to laugh together has made difficult times easier.
9. Instead of being judgmental about the practices of different cultures, it's more fun to try and adjust to what each culture deems acceptable when one is a visitor.
10. My eighty-year-old mother seems to be sixty because she's always trying something new, whether it is using a computer or doing yoga.

Sentence Variety Exercise
Answers will vary. Here are some possibilities.
1. I had to wear a uniform every single day, and you have no idea how much I hated it.
2. I've lived in five different countries, always trying to dress and act like the native people.
3. Although some people learn better from a manual or a teacher, I'm the kind of person who learns by doing, such as when I learned to ride a bicycle.
4. In contrast to what I've heard about some institutions in the United States, in my country teachers at the university level don't care whether or not students come to class.
5. Unfortunately my high school soccer team never won even one game.
6. Although I like to be alone during the week, I look forward to going out with my many friends on the weekend.
7. Maybe because I grew up in a modern twenty-two-story apartment building, I want to live in a traditional house.
8. Although I could never afford to visit Australia, I'd certainly like to visit there.
9. Some people like to listen to music when they're sad; whereas others like to listen when they're in a good mood.
10. Because my hometown is so small and boring, it doesn't even have a movie theater!

Title Exercises
I.   *Answers will vary.*

II. *Answers will vary. Here are some possibilities.*
1. Athletics Bring in the Money
2. Thousand of Cars and Tons of Pollution
3. A Room of My Own
4. Day Care Centers for the Elderly
5. The Championship Women's Soccer Team
6. Happy Children, Happy Adults
7. The Class I Never Missed
8. Study English and Expand Your Horizons
9. Esther: My Best Friend, My Companion, My Dog

Fragments and Run-On Sentences
Exercise 1
Here are some possible fragment and run on corrections.
1. F   ….watch, go to a good jeweler.
2. RO   …easy because it…
3. F   ….quiet is hard to find.
4. F   …trip is a good idea.
5. S
6. RO   …apartment, but I…..
7. F   There are twelve….
8. S
9. S
10. R   …directions, so she….

Exercise 2
Here are some possible fragment and run on corrections.

1. F   First, people who
2. S
3. F   friends, it is fun.
4. RO   example. When…
5. RO   there. I hope
6. RO   Spain. I think
7. S
8. F   something is a mistake
9. F   problems, I call a friend.
10. F   There are two…
11. F   …better than computers?
12. RO   countryside. I think…
13. F   kitchen, I screamed.
14. F   They learned a lot through…
15. F   it, I ask someone.
16. S
17. S
18. F   They took a summer job even though
19. F   beautifully, I help other people and know…
20. S

Parallelism

NOUNS	EXAMPLES	EXAMPLES
• ness	happiness	*sadness, shyness*
• (i)ty	community	*university, solidarity*
• th	width	*length, breadth*
• sion, tion	position	*information, registration*
• ism	Buddhism	*schism, impressionism*
• ure	architecture	*erasure, closure*
(ure can also indicate a verb)		
• ment	repayment	*government, enjoyment*

(ment can also indicate a verb)
- ude   gratitude   *solitude, magnitude*
- ence, ance   independence   *governance, credence*
- ship   friendship   *internship, leadership*
- ery, ary, ory   cemetery   *memory, bribery*

(ery, ary can also indicate an adjective)
- hood   neighborhood   *sisterhood, brotherhood*
- phy, gy, try   philosophy   *biology, geometry*
- inct/ct   precinct   *instinct, district*
- ess   address   *duress, stress*

(ess can also indicate a verb)

PEOPLE NOUNS
- ist, yst   chemist   *artist, analyst*
- er, or   doctor   *sailor, dancer*
- ess   hostess   *princess, stewardess*
- ian   librarian   *magician, vegetarian*
- ic   medic   *comic, cynic*

(ic can also indicate adjectives)
- eur   voyeur   *entrepreneur, voyeur*
- ant, ent   correspondent   *immigrant, claimant*

(ant, ent can also indicate adjectives)
- ect, ict   suspect   *architect, derelict*

(ect can also indicate verbs)

VERBS
- ize, yze   criticize   *memorize, theorize*
- ate, ete   refrigerate   *create, complete*

(ate can also indicate adjectives)
- ify   identify   *quantify, magnify*
- uish, ish   distinguish   *flourish, finish*

(ish can also indicate adjectives)
- en   lengthen   *widen, broaden*
- ute   dilute   *commute, compute*

(ute can also be an adjective
- ure   endure   *insure, capture*
- ose   oppose   *depose, suppose*
- ulge   indulge   *bulge, divulge*
- ict, uct   predict   *conflict, deduct*
- erse, earse   converse   *rehearse, traverse*
- end, ond   pretend   *correspond, respond*
- use   enthuse   *diffuse, confuse*
- erve   deserve   *preserve, serve*
- uce   produce   *reduce, introduce*
- ess   address   *redress, compress*
- uade, ade   persuade   *dissuade, degrade*

- ote   promote   *demote, connote*
- ave   behave   *engrave, save*
- age   encourage   *discourage, barrage*
- ect   reflect   *dissect, connect*
- ame   inflame   *tame, rename*
- ment   experiment   *compliment, government*
- oy   destroy   *employ, annoy*

ADJECTIVES

- ly   lovely   *friendly, neighborly*

(usually _ly signifies an adverb, but some nouns + ly= adjectives)

- less   careless   *useless, hopeless*
- ful   useful   *beautiful, careful*
- al   usual   *casual, mutual*
- ish   foolish   *selfish, sheepish*
- y   crazy   *sunny, happy*
- ary, ory   scary   *momentary, sedentary*
- ic   heroic   *energetic, athletic*
- ble, ible, able   incredible   *teachable, inflatable*
- ive, tive   passive   *successive, repetitive*
- ant, ent   dependent   *constant, blatant*
- ing, ed   interesting   *bored, frightening*
- ous, ious   religious   *serious, copious*
- ate, ete, ute   ornate   *obsolete, resolute*

WORD FORM EXERCISE

Fill in the missing part of speech:
Some forms have other options.

NOUN	PERSON WHO..	VERB	ADJECTIVE
creation	**creator**	create	**creative**
symbol	XXXXX	**symbolize**	**symbolic**
communication	**communicator**	**communicate**	communicative
art	**artist**	XXXXX	**artistic**
prediction	**predictor**	predict	**predictable**
execution	**executive**	execute	**executive**
correspondence	**correspondent**	**correspond**	**corresponding**
suspicion	**suspect**	suspicious	**suspect**
therapy	**therapist**	XXXXX	**therapeutic**
analysis	analyst	analyze	**analytic**
diagnosis	**diagnose**	**diagnostic**	**diagnostician**
education	**educator**	**educate**	educational
manipulation	**manipulator**	**manipulate**	**manipulative**
science	scientist	XXXXX	**scientific**
development	**developer**	develop	**developed**
competition	**competitor**	compete	**competitive**
immigration	immigrant	immigrate	XXXXX

popularity   XXXXX   popularize   **popular**

Parallelism Exercise I
Answers may vary. Here are some possibilities.
11. The apartment was beautiful, expensive, and **spacious**.
12. If you're going to use this recipe, you'll need a pepper, **an** onion, and **a** tomato.
13. Our teacher is interesting: she plays piano, writes poetry, and **paints watercolors**.
14. I always have **sung** and always will sing in the shower.
15. Please turn down the television or go to sleep.
16. Michael hopes his dedication, ability, and **consideration** will help him get the job.
17. Daniel is a happy child and **a sound sleeper**.
18. Jodie Foster is a great actress and **a good director**.
19. The books on the top shelf are older than **those on** the bottom shelves.
20. At the University of Pennsylvania, morning classes are far more popular than the afternoon **ones**.

Parallelism Exercise II
Answers may vary. Here are some possibilities.
11. I was in favor of either *painting the walls purple* or ***leaving them alone***.
12. Matt found what he needed in the desk: *a ruler, a pen*, and ***an old exam***.
13. The square was crowded with young tourists *studying their guidebooks, eating lunches from backpacks*, and ***taking pictures of each other***.
14. Moving to a new apartment means I'll have to *decide what to keep, what to give away*, and ***what to sell***.
15. During our coffee break we ate blueberry muffins that were *small* but ***delicious***.
16. The hats and coats were piled everywhere: *on the bed, on the chairs*, and even ***on the floor***.
17. Bonnie knew neither *what to say in her letter of application* nor ***how to express herself effectively***.
18. *Either the government will ban smoking in public buildings* or ***the people will revolt***.
19. Molly walked *across the square* and ***into the library***.
20. In the morning newspaper I *read that plans for a second airport are being considered* and ***noticed that the governor is opposed to the idea***.

Parallelism Exercise III
Answers may vary. Here are some possibilities.
11. Life is **simpler** and more convenient than **for** people who lived in the past.
12. I think neither spending time with one or two friends nor **being with** a large number of friends is preferable to being alone.
13. Some people say it is easy to get into but difficult to graduate **from** U.S. colleges or universities.
14. If the community would be bigger, it would be more comfortable and **convenient**.

15. A teacher can tell you what **is wrong** or which **way is better**.
16. I like to visit a lot of different foreign countries and to spend my time with the people there.
17. It helps people to get rid of something they don't want instead of throwing it away. **They should** give it to someone who needs and wants it.
18. I don't have to worry if the goods are **either** damaged or not worth anything.
19. The boss must decide **either** to hire new employees or retrain the current ones.
20. The unemployment figures for those under twenty-five in Manila is larger than **those in** Singapore.

Parallelism Exercise IV.
Answers may vary. Here are some possibilities.
11. After a day at the beach, the children came home tired, sunburned, and **hungry**.
12. Larry Bird was a quick, skillful, and **energetic** basketball player.
13. A good writer edits her work slowly, carefully, and **regularly**.
14. The English composition course contains short stories, a novel, and **poetry**.
15. When you write an essay, you should check each verb for **agreement**, tense, and form.
16. The airline allows passengers to take one, two or **three** suitcases.
17. My mother has been a waitress, a secretary, and **a teacher**.
18. My uncle spoke **with humor** and kindness.
19. I am hot, dirty, and **thirsty**.
20. The flavor of the strawberry yogurt is better than **the flavor of** the peach.

Parallelism Exercise V.
Answers may vary. Here are some possibilities.
11. We want to have a flower garden, but we don't know where to begin, how to proceed, or **which flowers to plant**.
12. The summer of 1950 was as hot **as**, if not hotter than any other in the last century.
13. **I know neither** what kind of computer he uses nor where he bought it.
14. I am afraid **of** and excited about taking the TOEFL.
15. Jared has sent resumes to graphic design firms in **both** Taipei and Hong Kong.
16. Chris is an affectionate husband, a dutiful son, and **a kind father**.
17. The shape of the rock, **the length**, and the color reminds me of a small elephant.
18. He danced gracefully, rhythmically, and **easily**.
19. Judy is a gifted woman: a biologist, **a carpenter**, and **a cook**.
20. Your job consists of arranging the books, cataloging the new arrivals, and **alphabetizing the brochures**.

Punctuation Exercise
1. Although Yutaka was absent**,** she e-mailed me for the homework.
2. There are three sections on the TOEFL exam**:** listening, structure, and reading
3. I improved my writing ability because I write **two** essays a day.
4. I got autographs from my three favorite movie stars: Meryl Streep, Jodie Foster, and Robin Williams.

5. Jean-Claude has taken several English classes; therefore, he is confident about his writing ability.
6. Luis Carlos, a Mexican, didn't want to take a class with **seven** other Mexicans.
7. Maria Paula, who comes from Colombia, explained in her essay why she prefers to live in a dorm.
8. Carmen's daughter was sick, so Carmen took her to the doctor.
9. **CORRECT**
10. **CORRECT**
11. After Diana came to one class, she never appeared again.
12. Luis speaks several languages: Portuguese, Spanish, English, and Italian.
13. I arrived on time for the test; however, I forgot my passport.
14. **CORRECT**
15. Bravo! If I call your name, you passed the entrance examination.

STUDENT ESSAY SCORES AND EXPLANATIONS
TOPIC 1
#1A
Score: 2
Noticeably inappropriate choice of words or word forms
Accumulation of errors in sentence structure and usage
Although good use of specifics, inadequate introduction, no background given; conclusion not related to the essay; not formatted correctly

#1B
Score: 3
Addresses the topic using somewhat developed details
Limited range of syntactic structures and vocabulary
Good examples; too repetitive; numerous preposition, plural errors

#1/C
Score: 4
Is generally well organized and developed
Demonstrates some syntactic variety and range of vocabulary
Very good examples; introduction needs work-- don't just repeat the prompt; some awkward phrasing

#1/D
Score: 3
Contains some errors that occasionally obscure meaning
Adequately organized and developed
Good vocabulary but repeats prompt too many times; specific examples needed; article errors

#1/E

Score: 2.5
Addresses the topic
Good length and specifics; numerous errors lower this score, including those of prepositions, pronouns, spelling, articles, word choice, and plurals

#1/F
Score: 2
Noticeably inappropriate choice or words or word forms
Accumulation of errors
Good conclusion, however numerous errors lower this score, including those of subject-verb agreement, prepositions, plurals, and word choice

#1/G
Score: 2
Long, but an accumulation of errors in sentence structure and usage
Good length; numerous errors lower this score, including those of spelling, word choice, prepositions, run-on sentences and sentence fragments

#1/H
Score: 4.5
Well organized and developed
Demonstrates syntactic variety and appropriate word choice
Addresses some parts of the task more effectively than others
Well-developed; conclusion needs development

#1/I
Score: 5
Effectively addresses the writing task
Demonstrates syntactic variety and appropriate word choice
Uses clearly appropriate details
A very effective essay--does everything right

#1/J
Score: 3.5
Displays some syntactic variety and range of vocabulary
Contains some errors that occasionally obscure meaning
Good length and examples; errors lower this score including those of subject-verb agreement and word choice

TOPIC 2
#2/A
Score: 3.5
Inconsistent facility with syntax and usage
Has some errors that occasionally obscure meaning

Very good specifics; some basic errors keep this essay from getting a higher score, including those of articles, subject-verb agreement, and plural as well as lack of paragraph organization

#2/B
Score: 3.5
Close to becoming a 4, but has some errors that occasionally obscure meaning
Very good specifics but introduction needs development; numerous errors lower this score, including those of run-on sentences, word choice, missing subject, prepositions, and spelling

#2/C
Score: 3.5
Uses some details to support a thesis
Inconsistent facility with syntax and usage
Very good specifics and interesting use of a proverb; errors lower this score, including those of double subject, spelling, and run-on sentences

#2/D
Score: 2
An accumulation of errors in sentence structure and usage.
A variety of examples, but introduction and conclusion lack development; numerous errors lower this score, including those of word choice, spelling, and prepositions

#2/E
Score: 3
Uses some details to support a thesis and illustrate an idea
Inconsistent facility with syntax and usage
Good specifics but lacking introduction and conclusion; numerous errors lower this score, including those of basic spelling and apostrophes

#2/F
Score: 1
Serious underdevelopment
Little detail
Serious and frequent errors in sentence structure and usage
Way too short; numerous errors lower this score, including those of fragments, participles, prepositions, articles, and verb tenses

#2/G
Score: 2
Lacks development
Accumulation of errors in sentence structure and usage

Don't use informal language in essays, such as "gonna"; numerous errors lower this score, including those of word order and word choice, run-on sentences, spelling, and articles

#2/H
Score: 3
Contains some errors that occasionally obscure meaning
Is adequately organized and developed except Par. 3 which has an organizational shift
Interesting introduction and specifics; numerous errors lower this score, including those of spelling, articles, apostrophes, participles, word order, and contractions

#2/I
Score: 3.5
Demonstrates fluency with vocabulary and syntax
Displays cohesion
A variety of specifics, effective conclusion ending with a question; errors lower this score, including those of count/non-count nouns and subject-verb agreement

#2/J
Score: 4.5
Is generally well organized and developed
Uses details to support a thesis/illustrate ideas
Wonderful specifics and examples; a few grammatical errors, including subject-verb agreement

TOPIC 3

#3/A
Score: 3.5
Addresses the topic well
Inconsistent facility with syntax and usage
Good specifics; numerous errors lower this score, including those of word choice, articles, and phrasing throughout

#3/B
Score: 2
Noticeably inappropriate word choice or word forms
Accumulation of errors in sentence structure and usage
Uses specifics, however numerous errors lower this score, including those of spelling, word choice, verb forms, sentence fragments, and subject-verb agreement

#3/C
Score: 3
Interesting ideas, but inconsistent facility with syntax and usage
Contains errors that occasionally obscure meaning

Compelling introduction; numerous errors lower this score, including those of articles, plurals, and awkward phrasing

#3/D
Score: 2
Inadequate development
Accumulation of errors in sentence structure and usage
Needs more than one paragraph--way too short; numerous errors lower this score, including those of subject-verb agreement, pronouns, and spelling

#3/E
Score: 1.5
Underdevelopment
Noticeably inappropriate choice of words or word forms
Accumulation of errors in sentence structure and usage
Single sentences aren't paragraphs--way too short; incorrect word choice throughout

#3/F
Score: 4.5
Uses details to support thesis and ideas
Addresses some parts of the task more effectively than others
Displays facility in language
Very good examples; syntax/usage is adequate; run-on sentence errors

#3/G
Score: 5
Although there are a few errors, in general demonstrates syntactic variety and appropriate word choice
Displays consistent facility in the use of language
Well-organized and well-argued; a weak paragraph, indentations would help

#3/H
Score: 0
Merely copies the topic
No essay here. Try never to copy the prompt anywhere in the essay.

#3/I
Score: 3.5
Displays progression
Uses some details to support thesis/illustrate idea
Inconsistent facility with syntax and usage
Good specifics, restates the arguments in the conclusion--don't say "the reasons above show"; errors lower this score including those of count/non-count nouns, and prepositions

#3/J

Score: 3
Inconsistent facility with syntax and usage
Uses some details to support thesis/illustrate idea
Good examples; numerous errors lower this score, including those of spelling, comparatives, articles, word choice and form, and abbreviations

TOPIC 4
#4/A
Score: 2.5
Addresses the topic
Accumulation of errors in sentence structure and usage
Uses somewhat developed examples and specifics but needs to be organized into paragraphs; numerous errors lower this score, including those of articles, prepositions, word form, participles, and verbs

#4/B
Score: 4
Generally well organized and developed
Displays facility in the use of the language
Some syntactic variety and range of vocabulary
Effective use of a question as a topic sentence; don't copy title from the prompt, some errors with semi-colons (;), spelling, and articles

#4/C
Score: 1
Accumulation of serious errors in sentence structure and usage
Serious and frequent errors in sentence structure and usage
Lack of development
Too short; numerous errors lower this score, including those of spelling, word order, verbs, fragments, and word choice

#4/D
Score: 2
Accumulation of errors in sentence structure and usage
Noticeably inappropriate choice of words or word forms
Indent paragraphs--needs multiple paragraphs and more development; numerous errors lower this score, including those of verbs, word choice, articles, spelling, and word form

#4/E
Score: 4.5
Effectively addresses the topic and task
Contains mirror lexical and grammatical errors
Well-argued with specifics, paragraphs need to be condensed and longer

#4/F
Score: 1

Serious and frequent errors in sentence structure and usage
Somewhat incoherent
Too short; illogical sentence connections

#4/G
Score: 3.5
Generally well-organized and well-developed
Contains some errors that occasionally obscure meaning
Good specifics; incomplete and illogical conclusion; errors lower this score, including those of capitalization, spelling, prepositions, and word choice

#4/H
Score: 5
Demonstrates syntactic variety and appropriate word choice
Displays facility in the use of language
A very effective essay-does everything right

#4/I
Score: 3.5
Adequately organized and developed
Uses some detail to support thesis and illustrate ideas
Contains some errors that occasionally obscure meaning
Inconsistent facility with syntax and usage
Good use of questions; errors lower this score, including those of subject-verb agreement, articles, and verb tenses

#4/J
Score: 3.5
Inconsistent facility with syntax and usage
Meaning occasionally obscured
Good paragraph development, focus and length; errors lower this score, including those of, word choice, word form, articles, and prepositions

TOPIC 5
#5/A
Score: 2.5
Accumulation of errors in usage but good conclusion
Good specifics, but no introduction, undeveloped paragraph 2; numerous errors lower this score, including those of word choice and word form

#5/B
Score: 3
Addresses the topic using examples and details
Inconsistent facility with syntax and usage

Good specifics; numerous errors lower this score, including those of subject-verb agreement, plurals, and prepositions

#5/C
Score: 3
Contains errors that occasionally obscure meaning
Inconsistent facility with syntax and usage
Uses details to support thesis and illustrate ideas
Good specifics but paragraphs need indentation; no real introduction; numerous errors lower this score, including those of articles, word choice, plurals, count/non-count nouns, and prepositions

#5/D
Score: 2
Accumulation of errors in sentence structure and usage
Noticeably inappropriate choice or words and word forms.
Uses examples, but inadequate paragraph development--don't end the essay with only a sentence; numerous errors lower this score, including those of word choice, articles, verbs, and prepositions

#5/E
Score: 2.5
Accumulation of errors in sentence structure and usage
Uses examples, but incomplete introduction, paragraphs need indentation; numerous errors lower this score, including those of sentence fragments and word choice

#5/F
Score: 4
Displays facility and range of vocabulary
Generally well-developed and organized
Good specific examples; numerous spelling and count/noncount noun errors

#5/G
Score: 1
Serious underdevelopment
Serious and frequent errors in sentence structure and usage
Ends too abruptly; numerous errors lower this score, including those of count/noncount nouns, spelling, subject-verb agreement, and word choice

#5/H
Score: 1
Serious underdevelopment
Serious and frequent errors in sentence structure and usage
Little detail

Numerous errors lower this score, including those of word form, subject-verb agreement, fragments, spelling, and missing words

#5/I
Score: 2.5
Uses some details to support thesis and illustrate ideas
An accumulation of errors in sentence structure and usage
Uses examples, but undeveloped conclusion; numerous errors lower this score, including those of subject-verb agreement, spelling, word choice and articles

#5/J
Score: 3.5
Uses appropriate examples
Inconsistent facility with syntax and usage
Undeveloped conclusion; errors lower this score, including those of plurals, spelling, articles, and prepositions

TOPIC 6
#6/A
Score: 3.5
Adequate but inconsistent facility with syntax and usage
Contains some errors that occasionally obscure meaning
Adequately organized and developed
Good specifics and organization; numerous errors lower this score, including those of plurals, articles, prepositions, and verb errors

#6/B
Score: 1.5
Inadequate organization and development
Noticeably inappropriate choice of words and word forms
Serious and frequent errors
Talk about your own country--when you personalize your writing, it's much more persuasive; numerous errors lower this score, including those of word forms, word choice, and subject-verb agreement

#6/C
Score: 1.5
Inadequate development and organization
Accumulation of serious errors in sentence structure and usage
Develop introduction; numerous errors lower this score, including those of verb tenses, spelling, word choice, word form, articles, plurals, count/ non-count nouns, prepositions, and word order

#6/D

Score: 1
Inadequate development and organization
Accumulation of serious errors in sentence structure and usage
Develop introduction and conclusion; numerous errors lower this score, including those of spelling, capitalization, plurals, word choice, prepositions, and articles

#6/E
Score: 3
Addresses the writing topic adequately but slights parts of the task
Inconsistent facility with syntax and usage
Good title, don't use informal language in essays, such as "wanna", develop paragraphs more; occasional errors, including those of subject-verb agreement and word form

#6/F
Score: 4
Addresses some parts of the task more effectively than others
Displays facility in the use of the language
Almost no errors with syntax or usage, but the length and lack of development prevent it from receiving a higher score

#6/G
Score: 5
Effectively addresses the task
Demonstrates syntactic variety and appropriate word choice
Good use of a question in the conclusion; well-argued and developed throughout

#6/H
Score: 1
Serious underdevelopment
Serious and frequent errors in sentence structure and usage
Little detail
Almost no errors with syntax or usage, but the length and lack of development prevent it from receiving a higher score

#6/I
Score: 5
Generally well developed and organized
Displays facility in the use of the language
Alternative organization (with numbering), but it works because points are developed in paragraph form with complete sentences

#6/J
Score: 4
Adequate but inconsistent facility with syntax and usage

Adequately organized and developed
Good conclusion; numerous errors lower this score, including those of phrasing and word choice

TOPIC 7
#7/A
Score: 3
Uses somewhat developed examples
Inconsistent facility with syntax and usage
Weak introduction which restates the prompt; numerous errors lower this score, including those of word-choice, articles, and plurals

#7/B
Score: 3
Contains some errors that occasionally obscure meaning
Inconsistent facility with syntax and usage
Interesting examples; numerous errors lower this score, including those of word form, count/noncount nouns, articles, verbs, and capitalization

#7/C
Score: 1
Serious disorganization and underdevelopment
Serious and frequent errors in sentence structure and usage
Organize the essay into paragraphs-- then organize each paragraph by ideas
Numerous errors lower this score, including those of spelling, sentence fragments, word form, plurals, and prepositions

#7/D
Score: 2
Accumulation of errors in sentence structure and usage
Noticeably inappropriate choice of words or word forms
Examples from personal experience work well; however, numerous errors lower this score, including those of plurals, prepositions, fragments, word form, and word choice

#7/E
Score: 5
Effectively addresses the task
Demonstrates syntactic variety and appropriate word choice
Consistent facility in the use of language
Impressive length and development

#7/F
Score: 3.5
Inconsistent facility with syntax and usage
Uses appropriate examples

Good title, details, length; errors lower this score, including those of verb tenses, capitalization, count/non-count nouns, word form, and prepositions

#7/G
Score: 1.5
Serious problem with focus
Serious disorganization and underdevelopment.
Frequent errors in sentence structure and usage
Underdeveloped; numerous errors lower this score, including those of pronouns, count/non-count nouns, and word choice

#7/H
Score: 1.5
Insufficient details to support or illustrate generalizations
Accumulation of errors in sentence structure and usage
Most of the sentences don't make sense

#7/I
Score: 2.5
Accumulation of errors in sentence structure and usage
Good length, questions, good examples; however, almost every sentence contains errors that lower this score, including those of spelling, word choice, word form, count/noncount nouns, run-on sentences, verbs, articles, and plurals

#7/J
Score: 3
Addresses the topic using explanations
Uses some details to support thesis/illustrate idea
Write from specifics rather than from generalizations
Good use of question in introduction; numerous errors lower this score, including those of word choice, spelling, participles, plurals, and word form

TOPIC 8
#8/A
Score: 2.5
Inconsistent facility with syntax
Accumulation of errors in sentence structure and usage
Title from the prompt doesn't add anything; numerous errors lower this score, including those of spelling, articles, subject-verb agreement, word choice, plurals, prepositions, and comparatives

#8/B
Score: 3.5
Inconsistent facility with syntax and usage
Contains some errors that occasionally obscure meaning
Uses details to illustrate an idea

Good details, but a thin introduction; has some awkward phrasings, word choice and plural errors

#8/C
Score: 2
Limited development in response to the topic
Contains some errors that occasionally obscure meaning
Underdeveloped introduction and conclusion; numerous errors lower this score, including those of comparative/superlative, word form, and run-on sentences

#8/D
Score: 5
Effectively addresses the writing task
Demonstrates syntactic variety and range of vocabulary
Although there are problems with the introduction, the essay is strong; occasional unobtrusive word choice errors

#8/E
Score: 1.5
Frequent errors in sentence structure and usage
Underdeveloped; numerous errors lower this score, including those of articles, word choice, prepositions, subject-verb agreement, and verbs

#8/F
Score: 3
Contains some errors that occasionally obscure meaning
Uses some details to support thesis and illustrate ideas
Adequate but inconsistent facility with syntax and usage
Good specifics; numerous errors lower this score, including those of articles, plurals, count/noncount nouns, word form, and word choice

#8/G
Score: 3
Undeveloped conclusion
Inconsistent facility with syntax and usage
Good examples, lack of focus in last body paragraph; numerous errors lower this score, including those of subject-verb agreement, word choice, and plurals

#8/H
Score: 3
Inconsistent facility with syntax and usage
Adequately developed and organized
Good specifics, but conversational tone doesn't work well, inadequate introduction; numerous errors lower this score, including those of word choice and phrasing

#8/I

Score: 4
Generally well organized and developed
Demonstrates some syntactic variety and range of vocabulary
Essay flows and has substantial examples; however, errors lower this score, including those of subject-verb agreement, articles, word choice, and word form

#8/J
Score: 5
Displays facility in the range of vocabulary
Uses details to support thesis/illustrate ideas
Alternative design listing points before the paragraphs could lower the score, but the fluidity and development of the arguments make it a 5

TOPIC 9
#9/A
Score: 3
Uses details to support thesis and illustrate idea
Inconsistent facility with syntax and usage
Good examples, but thin introduction and conclusion; numerous errors lower this score including those of phrasing, prepositions, and word choice

#9/B
Score: 3
Uses details to support thesis and illustrate ideas
Inconsistent facility with syntax and usage
Good specifics, but repeats phrase "children should be required..." too many times-- leaves the reader feeling writer hasn't said much

#9/C
Score: 4
Although the he/she him/her really gets in the way, the essay
is generally well-organized and developed
Demonstrates some syntactic variety and range of vocabulary
Good specifics, don't use he/she, his/her—pluralize everything (children/they/them/their)

#9/D
Score: 5
Displays consistent facility in the use of language
Demonstrates syntactic variety and appropriate word choice
Although only 2 paragraphs, includes a variety of examples and reads fluently, good title

#9/E
Score: 3
Addresses the topic using examples
Inconsistent facility with syntax and usage

Good specifics, but underdeveloped conclusion; numerous errors lower this score, including those of word choice, prepositions, and subject-verb agreement

#9/F
Score: 3.5
Adequately organized and developed
Inconsistent facility with syntax and usage
Interesting points, but underdeveloped introduction and conclusion and too many "!"s; errors lower this score, including those of word choice, plurals, prepositions, and phrasing

#9/G
Score: 2.5
Contains errors that occasionally obscure meaning
Inconsistent facility with syntax and usage
Uses some details to support thesis/illustrate ideas
Good length; numerous errors lower this score, including those of run-ons, plurals, subject-verb agreement, verb form, and tense

#9/H
Score: 4
Is generally well organized and developed
Displays facility in the use of the language
Uses details to support thesis/illustrate idea
Very good specifics, but underdeveloped conclusion; errors lower this score, including those of word choice and plurals

#9/I
Score: 3
Inconsistent facility with syntax and usage
Uses some details to support thesis/illustrate ideas
Good details; numerous errors lower this score, including those of word choice, articles, word order, word form, and plurals

#9/J
Score: 3
Inconsistent facility with syntax and usage
Addresses the topic and uses somewhat detailed examples
Good length, underdeveloped conclusion; numerous errors lower this score, including those of verb form, plurals, run-on sentences, non-count nouns, word form, and word choice